ENDORSEMENTS

This book does a great job of stressing the multi-faceted management issues facing the business owner today. It includes not only expert approaches to running the firm profitably, but delves into the owner's motives and views in defining success. The book includes timely topics such as "Internet Marketing", and "Diversity and Inclusion". The focus on "People" incorporates accepted principles of "quality", and "motivation". This book should appeal to both new and experienced business owners and managers.

- Augie Ridolfi
Former Wisconsin Technical College Marketing and Business Instructor, A.A., B.S., M.A.

Do you ever feel like you are working WAY too hard in your business? Most small business owners do. That's why every business owner needs a guide to grow a business with more peace, profitability and productivity which is why you must pick up a copy of *"Brilliant Breakthroughs For the Small Business Owner"*! This book will help you shine light on those areas in your business that you've been wanting to shift or change. And, while you are at it, pick up a few copies for your friends!

- Ursula Mentjes
Award-Winning Author of The Belief Zone, Selling with Intention, One Great Goal and Selling with Synchronicity

"Brilliant Breakthroughs" is exactly that. It has become one of the guidebooks to My American Dream. I have read their ongoing series and participated face-to-face in a "Brilliant Mind Summit". I must say this wonderful group of seasoned experts creates a powerful synergy of unique business and life, skills and perspectives, that promise peace, life, profit and success to those that embrace this refreshing, new path to living Your American Dream.

- James Patrick O'Malley
Founder, *MIOStream.net*

An imperative guide for every small business owner. It's filled with important information for anyone who wants to take their business to the next level. Kelly Andrew's chapter captures it perfectly, *If you haven't already implemented a strategic internet marketing plan, you've positioned yourself behind your competition.* This is a must read, you'll be glad you did.
- Nancy Lucchesi
The App Mama, Unleashed Mobile Apps & #1 Bestselling Author

"Brilliant Breakthrough for the Small Business Owner" is an amazing book. It is a fountain of wisdom that I find very uplifting and inspiring. The writing style is excellent, the use of stories makes the teaching come alive. Easy to read, easy to remember, and easy to apply.
- Chris Sanders, BBA

"Brilliant Breakthrough for the Small Business Owner" is a great read for those who currently own a business, or those who are aiming toward this goal. "Work hard, play hard" is one of my biggest philosophies, and a great manger/owner will recognize this. I found this to be true within the book when talking about a manager actually "doing research" on his/her employee. A great manger/owner should evaluate an employee's capabilities, AND capitalize off his/her strengths, which in essence, will not only help the employee, but the company as well.

The book also discussed the issue of "sloppy management." This was quite informative, as times have changed. What "used to be acceptable" is no longer. Again, managers and owners need to pay attention to the employee wants and needs. However, "little things do mean a lot," and this book illustrates the sources to ensure a retainable employee with having a great manager/owner. This book is educational, resourceful, and inspiring, and is a true fundamental to the library of any individual with entrepreneurial aspirations.
- Casey Block
HR Services Specialist II at Magnetek Inc.

Vision and intuition are the working aspects of Higher Consciousness. They work better in an environment of inspiration or "in spirit." In the work "*Higher Consciousness Creates Higher Profitability*", inspiration is at our fingertips, available when needed should we pop out of spirit or require an instant reboot.
- Roger Drummer
Diplomate Chinese Herbology, *www.Herbworks.com*

As an entrepreneur for almost 35 years, I learned the hard way that compassion positively impacts the bottom line. Susan has succinctly and eloquently made the case for embracing diversity and learning to be a compassionate leader. She provides actionable steps that any small business owner can put into practice for greater business success.
- Mary-Frances Winters
Founder and CEO, The Winters Group, Inc.
Global Diversity and Inclusion Consulting Firm

"*Brilliant Breakthroughs for the Small Business Owner*" is an awesome compilation of ready to implement advice from highly successful business owners and entrepreneurs. This time-tested and practical advice will enable you to take your business to the next level, with the rare addition of finding peace in your business!
- Kerrie Hoffman
Certified Business Coach, Digital Advisor, Keynote Speaker
FocalPoint Business Coaching

"*Higher Consciousness Creates Higher Profitability*" is a brilliant piece of work on the new success metrics by Nancy Clairmont Carr. The concepts she discusses are well researched and provide a variety of resources giving the reader many opportunities to go deeper. It is filled with hope and practical solutions which provide a roadmap to increased profitability, productivity, and optimum health. I have benefited significantly from these teachings professionally and personally.
- Louise Griffith MA
owner of **www.OneShiningLight.com** and author of *You Are Worth It: 52 Weeks of Honoring, Loving and Nurturing Your Soul.*

As a decades-long organizational psychologist, these things I know for sure:
"What you feel will become your success; How you treat others will become your legacy; and Where you focus will become where you land. How can those answers NOT be Joy, Abundance and Freedom? Let *Higher Consciousness Creates Higher Profitability* show you how to find your own path to each."
- Dr. Mia Mulrennan
I/O Psychologist, CHRO, and Owner: Rave-Worthy Consulting and Publishing Group

As a small business owner for over 14 years, I've had to learn the hard way to become successful. Had I had access to this book when I started, I would have been able to grow so much faster and with more ease. This book is a must have for any small business as it encompasses so many aspects of the how-tos. What's more is that the authors write from such a heartfelt space. What a gift!
- Debbie Leoni
Fearless Living Coach and Speaker

I have the honour of writing the forward to Becky Norwood's first book and the pleasure of watching her grow from that day into the successful book publishing expert she is today. Becky's talent lies not only in her extensive knowledge and understanding of the publishing industry, but also in her warm and giving personality, combined with an astute business sense. Becky is a rare find, a gem of outstanding quality.
- Sue Ferreira
President of Wisdom To Wealth Mastery

I love how each chapter is filled with small business expertise that is so desperately needed AND extremely current! The authors not only brought their own expertise, they also interviewed other experts to make sure that they included what is happening RIGHT NOW in the business world. This isn't the same old recycled business info that is readily available everywhere. This truly is a mind-opening collection of Fresh (as in current) Perspectives straight from today's experts.

- Lori Bonaparte
Personal Development Coach
Founder of ***www.TrueYouInAction.com***

Management 101 - this chapter is a concise summary of the simple truths that many of us lose focus of. Each of us has the capacity to be a great leader - and Clive's roadmap on how to do that is spot on. Making management theory complex doesn't make it better. I've found myself coming back to Clive's straight-forward learnings again and again. If every leader adhered to even half of the lessons in this chapter, they couldn't help but be a better leader - and drive better cultures.

- Steve Baue
President / CEO of ERC: Counselors and Consultants

This book is critical for the forward thinking, small business entrepreneur! Nancy Clairmont Carr is one of them! Her contribution, *Higher Consciousness Creates Higher Profitability,* helps us clearly see that creativity, passion for work and productivity come from daily care of your mind, emotions and body. Daily self-care connects you to your intuition which is accessed from your spirit—the most powerful creative force there is! Nancy gives suggestions such as energy work, meditation and whole-body self-care to open up your intuition, bringing you to your best self and optimal ideas. Her approach is not the old business model. It is what's needed to help influencers move forward during this era of great change.

- Maureen Higgins
MA, Alternative counselor, coach & energy practitioner
www.WingsofFreedom1.com

"Breakthroughs for the Small Business Owner" holds truth for not just entrepreneurs but also those aspiring to any area of business, as I find the lessons in this book are applicable to a wide variety of success-oriented individuals. As a student, the tips for

collaboration and motivation have impacted the way I approach my professors and internships!
- **Claire O'Malley**
Advertising/Public Relations, Loyola University Chicago

Of all the four pillars, the **PEOPLE** *pillar resonated the most with me. I love the way Susan* McCuistion builds the business case for diversity even for small businesses. Using historical references and case studies, she methodically explains how companies build diversity debt. My belief about compassion as a key driver at the workplace is even more strong now, with Susan's take on compassionate diversity. A recommended read for any small business owner.
- **Shrivallabh Kulkarni**
Small business owner, India

Kelly E. Andrew has done a phenomenal job introducing and laying out the life-cycle stages for the wildly successful Inbound Marketing strategy. If you're a business owner and not currently implementing Inbound marketing, you need to read this, otherwise you're behind in the game. I gained a lot from this chapter even as a 20-year Internet marketing veteran.
- **Greg Bernhardt**
Owner of ***www.physicsforums.com***

Having recently entered into the world of small business, *"Brilliant Breakthroughs for the Small Business Owner"* is chock-full of helpful tips and down to earth advice that anyone can learn from; small business owner or not. The tips in this book have helped me to realign my goals so I can start reaching new levels of success and achieve the mission that I have set out for my business. I highly recommend this as a read for any small business owner looking to avoid the busyness trap and start running towards their dream.
- **Nick Myers**
Founder & Creative Director, RedFox Creative

This is a fresh perspective on Management 101 without assuming a "one size fits all" solution to every management opportunity.

I appreciate the approach, which resembles a discussion with a respected colleague or mentor. A great reminder that each situation requires mindful thought and a response to fit the situation. A call to action at the conclusion of each concept automatically challenges me to apply it to my daily life!
- **Carolyn Schultz**
Project Manager
MS Management & Organizational Behavior; PMP

The research shows there is significant impact from all that we think, feel, and do on our biology, and our ability to live happily and embodied in our own values around success. The featured authors in this book are spot on in highlighting how the 4 Performance Pillars are foundational for creating a profitable business in a purposeful, inspired, and healthy way.

Nancy Clairmont Carr's chapter, *Higher Consciousness Creates Higher Profitability*, beautifully highlights the impact of increased consciousness on our ability to work creatively, inspired, and intuitively, while removing anything in the way of our abundance! I love how she has healed and shifted her own beliefs around hard work and life balance to create a life of flow, wellness, balance, and most importantly, happiness! She is a radiant example of what she teaches. This book provides awesome truth and support for small business owners and leaders in any area.
- **Rev. Dr. Rachel Wetzsteon**
Author of "Radiantly Free: Recreating Life & Health from the Radiance of You" and host of the REV with Rachel podcast

Small business owners are required to wear many hats. They are entrepreneur, employer, accountant, HR/benefit specialist, sales/marketer, and strategic planner all at the same time and with expectations to excel in each discipline. Successful SBOs learn to do this, how can you? The book "Brilliant Breakthroughs for the Small Business Owner" reveals expert guidance and answers many questions.
- **John Dedrick**
Retired President & CEO, West Bend Mutual Insurance Company

I was lucky enough to be a contributing author in the 2017 edition of this #1 bestseller. And the 2018 version doesn't disappoint. Chockfull of wisdom for the small business owner, this book needs to be on your bookshelf. If you don't have the 2017 edition, you should add it as well. Kudos to Maggie Mongan and all the contributing authors for another sterling effort.
- David Wallace
Chief Status Quo Prosecutor, Bay Ridge Consulting Group, LLC & Amazon #1 Bestselling Author

This book effectively describes the importance of culture in the workforce. It gives real-life examples of how basic management styles can empower your most important resource...your employees. I recommend all managers (new or experienced) read this book and take a moment to reflect how well they implement these tools to ensure a profitable productive business.
- Mrs. Laurie Schlitt,
CEO/Executive Director, Volunteer, Board Member, Wife and Mother

Today's small business owners can't look at outdated success manuals. Those strategies were unique to the time, people, and industry. Thankfully they can achieve similar success by accessing their higher level of consciousness, as described in the work *"Higher Consciousness Creates Higher Profitability"*.

Our best ideas and solutions come when we prepare ourselves for the moment. Isn't it interesting how successful people share similar habits: meditation, nutrition, exercise, and sleep. They create the energy needed to inspire the right idea, at the right time. The entire book, *Brilliant Breakthroughs for the Small Business Owner,* shows how to become the leader your business needs!"
- Adam Wallschlaeger, Certified Business Coach

This important work shows us the importance of "Making heart connections" in the business world as a critical, beneficial

ingredient for companies that want to speak to their customers in lasting ways. With compelling examples, it will show you how companies can meaningfully connect with your employees, customers, and community. What a fresh dose of practical wisdom from its authors!"
- **Jane Hyun**
Author, *Breaking the Bamboo Ceiling* and Co-Author, *Flex/The New Playbook for Managing Across Differences*
Founder & President, Hyun & Associates, Inc. Leadership Consulting
www.hyunassociates.com

Becky Norwood has that rare gift, the combination of heart and head, that allows her to see the big picture and the small details at the same time. She understands how to craft a message so it will resonate with the heart...without losing track of the small things that will make or break a book launch. As a publisher and as a person, Becky is an angel, a *brilliant* angel!
- **Everett O'Keefe**
#1 International Bestselling Author and Founder of Ignite Press.

Sometimes we all need a "swift kick" or fresh perspective to look at HOW we're doing our business and how we can make it better. If you're a small business owner and find yourself stuck, or just working much harder than you should be, there are some great pointers and wisdom in these pages.
- **Greg Nicholson**
Founder, Elevate Business & #1 Bestselling Author

It is about time that we moved beyond all the noise that tells you how to get rich quick in building a successful, sustainable small business. This book gives the reader the foundations to build and grow a small business. This book provides a holistic approach to building you AND your business.

Nancy Clairmont Carr's chapter "*Higher Consciousness Creates Higher Profitability*" takes the law of attraction and abundance mindset to a new level of thinking and application. Having owned

my own successful small business for the last 28 years and having had to discover these concepts the hard way, I know the power that Nancy speaks of in her chapter. At last, we can shorten the learning curve and get to faster profitability.
- **Cheryl Leitschuh**
"Yoda" for Small Business Women, Straight Talk for Smart Business Women

Regardless of which stage you are in your business, this book is a must-read to lead, inspire your team to live the values of your organizations, and achieve superior results over the long term. The practical and realistic advice, techniques, and strategies shared by the experts can be used right away to provide immediate impact as we work towards developing a stronger, more productive and profitable business; and help us keep our minds in the game.
- **Elsie González**, M.S.
Owner at Motiva Consulting

This book is a must-read for entrepreneurs and business owners who are serious about being profitable, successful and having more joy in their business endeavours. This book will help business owners increase success and decrease the stress of running a thriving business.
- **Charmaine Hammond**
CSP, MA Professionals Speaker, Author and Collaboration Expert

It's in the heart of every small business owner to bring their brilliance to the marketplace and make a positive impact on the people they serve. But that cannot be achieved without the small business owner being enlightened with fresh perspectives to help them adapt to the way today's society thinks, works, and plays. The Practicing Experts, who authored this book, open your eyes to a whole new way of thinking and conducting business. Alignment between these new thought patterns and work strategies provide the readers of this book a modern pathway to growing their business and achieving success in today's world.
- **Dave Rebro**
#1 Bestselling Author & The Technology Therapist

This book is a "must read" for managers and business owners. Each chapter contains practical workplace strategies, written by authors with experience finding solutions to business challenges. You will be inspired to self-reflection, and then to action. Then keep it nearby. You will go to it again and again, as a helpful guide to grow and manage your business.
- John F. Duwell
J.D., C.P.C.U.
Retired EVP and Chief Legal Officer

Brilliant Breakthroughs for the Small Business Owner, Volume 2, is great! The authors are obviously small business owners themselves. They are "Practicing Experts™", in the words of Maggie Mongan, the compiler and publisher of the book.

Interview shows have long been my favorite television. Not the late-night talk shows, rather the ones with real depth, like *Charlie Rose* and *Inside the Actors Studio*. The authors of *Brilliant Breakthroughs* show the same kind of depth as guests on the interview shows. They are in business because they love what they do. And they love the way they do it, the way they serve others. And they›ve learned to do it profitably. Their insights and convictions shine through and through.

The style of the book reminds me of those interview shows I've loved. Experts in their niches expounding on their passions. Reading the book, it almost feels as though you have friends and mentors talking to you, one on one. Well done!
- Keith Klein
CEO, On Your Mark, LLC

BRILLIANT BREAKTHROUGHS
FOR THE SMALL BUSINESS OWNER

Fresh Perspectives on Profitability,

People, Productivity, and Finding

Peace in Your Business

Compiled By

Maggie Mongan

Brilliant Breakthroughs, Inc.

Milwaukee, WI

BRILLIANT BREAKTHROUGHS FOR THE SMALL BUSINESS OWNER:
Fresh Perspectives on Profitability, People, Productivity, and Finding Peace in Your Business - Volume 2

PAPERBACK ISBN-9781730749780
eBOOK ISBN-13: 978-0-9994375-3-7

Library of Congress 2018912690

First Published in the USA in 2018 by Brilliant Breakthroughs, Inc.

Publishing Advisor: Spotlight Publishing™

Book Cover: Maggie Mongan with Angie Analya

Interior Design: fiverr.com/weformat (www.vanzzsolutions.com)

Group Portrait Photographer:
Stacy Kaat Photography www.StacyKaat.com

For information contact:

Brilliant Breakthroughs, Inc.
www.BrilliantBreakthroughs.com

DEDICATION

**This book is dedicated to Small Business Owners.
You are our economy's accelerant.**

Contents

ACKNOWLEDGMENTS

Above all else, to the love of my life, Chris. You captured my heart over 35 years ago. I appreciate how we have created our own balancing dance of leading and following one another. Your patience and loving support through this special project exemplifies the exceptional man you are. Thanks for holding me and making me laugh through the bumps of this journey!

There are many people to thank for co-creating this extraordinary book. Thank you, beloved contributing author team, for delivering high-quality chapter content and making this accomplishment one to remember. Big hugs to The Community of Brilliant Practicing Experts™, who have traveled with us this past year. Without you, this would have been more difficult to accomplish. Your wisdom and actions are appreciated!

Special thanks to Nancy Lucchesi for creating an excellent mobile app: **BrilliantBizBook** for us to serve Small Businesses. Jake Nawrocki for keeping our weekly podcast: **Brilliant Breakthroughs** showing up on the airwaves. Stacy Kaat for capturing us shining brightly in our 2018 Author Team photo. Dave Rebro for helping me simplify many moving parts! Deepest appreciation to Webmaster Keith Klein for keeping everything happening correctly behind the scenes!

Additional gratitude to our Advising Publisher, Becky Norwood of Spotlight on Your Business. Becky is a consummate professional and wise guide. She had such grace through this learning curve. What a ride!

Too many teachers, mentors, colleagues, and friends to mention this time! I acknowledged many of you in Volume 1 of this series. There are so many of you, who hold a special place in my heart. We always welcome each of you to our table.

Brilliant Breakthroughs for the Small Business Owner:

Fresh Perspectives on Profitability, People, Productivity, and Finding Peace in Your Business

INTRODUCTION

THE BRILLIANT QUESTION:
Maggie, why are you writing a book?

When speaking with George A. Santino, a retired Microsoft Partner, and Serial Entrepreneur, he stated, "The American Dream is alive and well. You can start at the bottom and work hard. If you do, anything is achievable" (personal communication, July 7, 2017). I wholeheartedly agree with George, who is the personification of The American Dream.

THE BRILLIANT ANSWER:
Contemporary business requires small business owners to think and act differently than they did in the 20th century. Small businesses of the 21st century must find the balancing act between traditional business basics and unconventional techniques. This isn't as easy as it appears. There is a noticeable disconnect between the support system (trainers, coaches, mentors, etc.,) for small business and what small business owners need to survive and thrive.

This book shares fresh perspectives on profitability, people, productivity, and peacefulness, for you to experiment with by applying them to your business. Our goal is to support small business owners in finding their potential solutions to develop their winning formula for business success.

THE BRILLIANT REASON:
The American Dream is a viable reality in this century. It provides equal opportunity for all who pursue their dream. Those who

create right actions, which are spurred from right thoughts, will reap the rewards.

Many people will start a business. Most are *wantrepreneurs* (those who talk about business ownership but don't do the work to build and deliver a successful business). This book is created for those who are seriously committed to doing the work and gaining prosperity. Ready for the good news? You can stop banging your head against the wall and quit working all hours of the night. This book is filled with all sorts of fresh perspectives for you to experiment with to find your personal secret to success.

In *The Entrepreneur's Solution*, Mel Abraham wrote, "This country was built on principles of entrepreneurialism, equity, self-determination, and opportunity. Fulfilling our potential, as individuals and as a nation is simply a matter then of reawakening that innate spirit" (Abraham, 2015, p. 3). The American Dream evolved through settlers, who became entrepreneurs and small business owners. These early founders of The American Dream started their businesses out of necessity. Some thrived to build great businesses, while others dwindled. All had the entrepreneurial spirit. Those who excelled learned how to master small business success.

Let's fast-forward to this century. If you are a seriously committed and growth-focused Small Business Owner, we know you're seeking new ways to:

- become more profitable
- develop better quality working relationships with your team and others
- explore and experiment with new productivity practices and tools
- find more peace within your business.

Why? For you to build a profitable business and experience a more joyful and fulfilling life. We get it, and you do too! We wrote this book to share some of our best practices and unconventional techniques to successfully grow YOUR Business. It's amazing what comes out of the mouths of Practicing Experts when they are sharing their wisdom.

The 21st century requires Small Business Owners (SBOs) to think and work differently to gain wins. When you are playing a new board game, you usually read the rules to the game, don't you?

Sure you do. Why? You want to assure you improve your probability of winning. Business is the same. There are basic rules for all businesses. We know these rules support strong business.

What's the difference in the rules for small business success between last and this century? The internet and technological advancement. Good, bad, or indifferent, the internet has both helped and hindered small business success.

The internet has created endless opportunity for SBOs to share their offerings with the world. Conversely, the internet is filled with a plethora of information – useful, accurate, and inaccurate. In a short period of time, humankind has become gluttons of information.

Even with the technological advancements, many business basics are still required. In the 21st century, businesses still need marketing, sales, customers, systems, accounting, etc., for business operations to run effectively and efficiently. Technology adds another layer of simplicity and complexity to any small business operation.

Technology provides opportunities for:

- greater reach to expand a business's marketplace
- around-the-clock promotion via social media and online advertising
- more information to consume
- efficiencies
- perpetual distractions via *Bright Shiny Objects* popping up
- more Experts and UN-Experts are vying for your attention and money.

A new learning curve and balancing act for this century's SBO is far different than last century. It is a necessity for small business to swiftly secure success. Today's SBOs are required to immediately work with experts to shave years off their learning curve to secure their position in the marketplace. When SBOs take consistent actions to secure profitability, they move beyond surviving.

Today's wide-reaching arm of the internet introduces you to an infinite number of service providers to help you grow your business.

Warning: All providers are not created equally.

There are plenty of experts in the marketplace. Experts are experienced and knowledgeable in a particular topic. Experts are masterful because they are practiced in their expertise or focused specialty.

Today's SBO has plenty of experts and UN-experts approaching them. The UN-experts are in strong force and you've probably engaged with them – vowing to never again. The UN-expert is usually an expert at online marketing, but not an expert at whatever it is they're offering. They promote well and engage you enough to secure your purchase. Unfortunately, their expertise stops there. They don't deliver at an expert level whatever the topic is you bought. The UN-expert tends to keep their customers in a state of mediocrity or perpetual need for their services.

Good news! You don't have to settle for UN-experts. In fact, a group of us believes SBOs deserve much better than what the marketplace is commonly providing for support. Over the past two years, I have been selecting and vetting Practicing Experts. There are many Practicing Experts in the marketplace. Those who are willing to openly share how they blend their best practices and unconventional techniques to build winning strategies and practical tactics to amplify their business success are collaborating authors of this book.

Some of you may ask, "How do you know they're practicing experts, Maggie?" For almost a decade, I had the honor of being trained to be one to the industry's top performers, as an Executive Recruiter and Certified Senior Account Manager, specializing in placing Change Agents into organizations. Additionally, I've coached executives, SBOs, non-profit leaders, and other professional coaches for 20+ years. Last, I've been coaching SBOs for 15 years.

In the late 1990s, I started saying to all the Change Agents I was recruiting, "It's all about being an Agent of Change; not an Agent for Change." Over the years, I've refined this to, "Don't be an agent for change; be the agent OF change." As you can see, I am an advocate for appropriate change. How successful business was conducted in the 1990s and even 2000s isn't enough for today's small business. Change – appropriate change, is required for SBOs to succeed in business. Most SBOs already know this, but they are unsure what to do about it.

This perplexed me too! For the past six years, I've been seeking a solution. What is it you ask? You're reading it. I invited other experts to build a collaborative Community of Brilliant Practicing Experts™ to bring proven and effective fresh perspectives to Small Business Owners. To reveal our commitment level to you, we started a mobile app named *BrilliantBizBook* to support the readers of our book series. This book is the second book in the #1 Bestselling Annual Business Book Series designed to continue giving you different fresh perspectives to experiment with throughout the years.

All this has me singing the lyrics to the original *Ghostbusters* movie, "Who ya gonna call?" Hopefully, your answer isn't the slick marketers who will be ghosted next year. Rather, it's to engage with Brilliant Practicing Experts™ once you read their chapter. Why? This is how you will learn this century's winning formula of success.

Tip: Most, not all, UN-experts keep you in a state of mediocre busy-ness work. Why? When you only gain mediocre results, you still need them and will pay them more money to get additional mediocre results. Even though they say otherwise, many UN-experts want you to become only moderately successful.

I know, their behavior is not acceptable! Since we are a society that is addicted to being busy, this has become a perfect storm for many online marketers. Unfortunately, they are capitalizing on this and robbing you of your profitability, productivity, and finding peace in your business.

What's the better approach to 21st century small business success?

Blending Best Practices and technology to create unconventional approaches. Why? Guided by a Brilliant Practicing Expert™, this approach will provide you and your business unconventional results. Brilliant Practicing Experts™ focus on attracting customers (catch), teach you what you need to learn so you can do it independently from them (feed), then encourage you to experiment with your new teachings (release), and are available if you need assistance (support).

Remember: Some information on the internet is accurate and some is inaccurate. If it was about having access to information, wouldn't we all be rich, physically fit, and beautiful by now?

Clue: For the first time in history, we are currently experiencing an information surplus and a deficit of application.

Your business's success is dependent upon you (1) securing the appropriate information, and (2) learning how to appropriately apply it to your business's circumstances.

Today's SBO has a variety of options available of what to offer and a myriad of delivery alternatives. Some techniques better support certain types of expertise or customers. There is a plethora of success options to consider; yet, some might not support your business as well as others.

How do you learn which approach is best? Experiment. The United States of America was founded by immigrants who learned how to support themselves through entrepreneurial activities and developing small businesses. Those who practiced until they succeeded, built growing business. Eventually, some of them became founding businesses of America. These early founders of The American Dream understood the value of experimenting.

Everything was new to these early business experimenters. The Founders of American Business needed to swiftly try new approaches and learn which ones did or didn't deliver favorable gains. Those who found success strategies and techniques became prosperous. Those who didn't find business success may not have survived.

The 21st century may not have mortality attached to business success for most, as it did in the 16th and 17th century, but it still requires an unwavering commitment from the SBO. The commitment is one of first surviving and then thriving. This requires and invites SBOs endless exploring and experimenting to find favorable results for their business. Those who persistently take action win. Those who take action on the right things win BIG.

Gary Vaynerchuk, high profile American Serial Entrepreneur often referred to as GaryVee, is known by his followers for advocating action. He frequently references hustling. Often, you hear him say things like, "Work, that's how you get it", "Stop crying; keep hustling", or "Without hustle, talent will only carry you so far". Vaynerchuk is a proponent of taking action and experimentation to shorten an entrepreneur's learning curves.

On a July 7, 2017 Instagram Live, GaryVee said, "Entrepreneurship emerges as culture" (*https://www.instagram.com/garyvee/*). The culture, he elaborated about is one of action. He encouraged *wantrepreneurs* to be practical and appropriately prepare for their business by gaining tutelage before and during entrepreneurship. He also emphasized a business's success rate is improved through experimentation – just like the early founders of The American Dream.

Typically, right thoughts and right actions deliver favorable results. Some, not all, of the Best Practices of corporations are favorable for small business success. Conversely, there are many strategies, techniques, mindsets, and behaviors that would become unfavorable if scaled to larger organizations.

I still notice many former corporate employees, who were downsized during this century's Great Recession, have become Small Business Owners. They're either trying to behave *corporate* in a small business setting or act as if they are hyperallergic to anything which *feels* it came from their former corporate setting. I encourage former corporate folks to quit sabotaging themselves and fully step into small business ownership with a clean slate to improve your business's success rate.

Caution: Similar to corporate settings, the behaviors which secured your promotion aren't the same actions and behaviors that will help you break into the next level of success – there's different game plans for each level. The rules change when you change levels. The game is played differently to excel in each new level. Small business success doesn't promote its business owners. Instead, it secures scalability or another level of expansion for the business. Each new level has its own rules for you to successfully master.

NOW WHAT?

Are you a committed Small Business Owner who seeks ways to make your small business more profitable and peace-filled so you can further step into living your potential? If so, you are going to enjoy this book. Figure 1 is a photo of our 2018 Brilliant Practicing Experts™ Author Team.

Figure 1.

Brilliant Practicing Experts™ 2018 Team of "Brilliant Breakthroughs for the Small Business Owner: Fresh Perspectives on Profitability, People, Productivity, and Finding Peace in Your Business (Volume 2)".

Source: Brilliant Breakthroughs, Inc. Photo taken by Stacy Kaat Photography.

This extra-ordinary team has created this book (2018 version) for you to explore and experiment with fresh perspectives to improve your business's performance.

We have organized our chapter topics into **The 4 Performance Pillars for Small Business Success**™ model: Profitability, People,

Productivity, and Peacefulness. Over the past 2 decades of serving businesses, I've noticed all business activities can be categorized into these 4 categories or Performance Pillars. The size and industry of a business doesn't alter this model.

When you review **The 4 Performance Pillars for Small Business Success**™ model (see Figure 2), you will see The 4 Performance Pillars in the center. I have added two columns for you to discern where you or your business may need to strengthen a Performance Pillar.

Figure 2.

THE 4 PERFORMANCE PILLARS FOR SMALL BUSINESS SUCCESS™

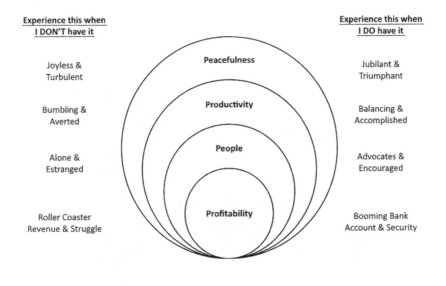

Experience this when I DON'T have it		Experience this when I DO have it
Joyless & Turbulent	Peacefulness	Jubilant & Triumphant
Bumbling & Averted	Productivity	Balancing & Accomplished
Alone & Estranged	People	Advocates & Encouraged
Roller Coaster Revenue & Struggle	Profitability	Booming Bank Account & Security

Source: Courtesy of Brilliant Breakthroughs Inc., Simplify Small Business Success Program:
https://academy.brilliantbreakthroughs.com/

The column on the left, *Experience this when I DON'T have it* column gives you key words to assess if you are lacking (or not). The column on the right, *Experience this when I DO have it* column reveals if you have been working these areas of your business effectively. The key is to fortify each of these 4 Performance Pillars.

The following is a brief description of each of The 4 Performance Pillars.

Performance Pillar 1: Profitability

The primary determinant of Business Success is if your business is profitable. We train on these topics: financials, product development, sales, marketing, branding, operations, business models, your business's purpose-vision-mission for alignment, and anything related to profit.

Performance Pillar 2: People

People are what makes the world go around – and your business too. We train on these topics: effective networking, social media, team development, employees, your business's ideal customer, business allies (joint ventures, etc.), customers, and anything related to relationship building and people.

Performance Pillar 3: Productivity

Productivity practices can make or break a business. Simplifying your activities may be easier than what you're making it out to be. We train on these topics: time management (which really doesn't exist), simplifying techniques, automated systems, tech and apps to support us being more effective and efficient, and anything related to productivity.

Performance Pillar 4: Peacefulness

Peacefulness is a possibility when you have a mindful and profitable business. It isn't necessary to polarize peace and profit. Peace is one of the elusive elements of Business Success that doesn't need to be far-fetched. We train on these topics: self-management, balanced leadership and self-leadership, utilizing core values, daily practices, mindset, overall well-being, and anything related to peaceful prosperity.

Note: The 4 Performance Pillars for Small Business Success™ model is one of the Small Business's Evolution. It illustrates how Profitability anchors your business. Profit is always at the forefront. Since people decide whether to make a purchase or not, People is the next essential ring surrounding Profit. There are many moving parts that need attention while conducting business. Learning how to be effective and efficient are essential; thus, Productivity is the next ring after People. The more People involved, the more Productivity becomes a focus. People don't want to, nor should they, work in an unpeaceful workplace. Peace is the outer ring, which encapsulates all the other activities.

At first glance, many SBOs will see this as I described. At another glance, SBOs may say the sequence could be reversed. This is the beauty of this model. Depending on your current business performance focus, you could move any one of the 4 pillars around since each pillar integrates with all the others. **Hint:** I do suggest you work the model as described because you can have all the peace you'd like to have, but if you don't have profit, your peace and business won't be lasting too long.

It's our intention to help you explore fresh perspectives in each of **The 4 Performance Pillars for Small Business Success**™ to have brilliant breakthroughs for yourself, as well as your business's performance.

WHAT'S NEXT?

Before our Brilliant Practicing Experts™ bring you the WOW! in each of their chapters, please take a moment to learn how the book is designed for you to use as a guide. Also, please engage with us on our mobile app: **BrilliantBizBook**. You may be surprised what we have there. Have some fun experimenting and shining brightly!

Brilliant Breakthroughs for the Small Business Owner:

HOW TO USE THIS BOOK

This book is a compilation or anthology of 8 authors, who are Brilliant Practicing Experts™, willing to share their wisdom and winning formulas with you, the small business owner.

As you read the book, you may notice it feels as if you are reading 8 different books. Why? Each chapter was written by a different author. Out of respect to each author, who has already created their customer base and a communication style within their marketplace, we honored their communication style throughout their chapter. We prefer this approach because we want you to know exactly what to expect when you reach out to engage with each of our authors.

This book is designed to introduce and wisdom-share fresh perspectives, so you may create some brilliant breakthroughs for yourself and your business's performance.

Use this book as a guide over the next year. Whatever you do, please don't only read this book and put it on the shelf! Instead, we invite you to experiment with the new ideas presented here. Learn and apply, practice and tweak, and then when you have a new best practice, smile and share your good news with us!

What you won't find in this book is advertisements. No one will be pitching their products or services to you. Our goal is to wisdom-share fresh perspectives for small business success.

BOOK LAYOUT:

This book's layout is organized via *The 4 Performance Pillars for Small Business Success*™ described in the Introduction.

PERFORMANCE PILLAR 1: PROFITABILITY

Chapter 1:

The Inbound Pipeline to Success
by Kelly E. Andrew

Surprise! Internet Marketing Isn't Just About Blogs, Social Media Posts, and E-Newsletters. When You Focus Your Efforts On An Inbound Strategy, You'll Get Better Results.

If you assume the internet is the least personal place to market your business, you're wrong. Growing businesses use online tools and technology to build solid relationships with their prospects and customers. This chapter will help you understand the importance and urgency of establishing a strategic internet marketing plan. In it, you'll learn:

- What components make up the Inbound Marketing Strategy
- Why you must establish your strategy *before* executing tactics
- How to track your success and ROI with valuable data-points
- Why it's important to integrate your sales and marketing efforts
- The value in starting today

Perfect for business owners and marketing managers, *The Inbound Pipeline to Success* demonstrates how to build and execute a successful internet marketing strategy, no matter what industry you're in.

Chapter 2:

Higher Consciousness Creates Higher Profitability
by Nancy Clairmont Carr

Typically, small business owners are all work and no play. They should be able to express their purpose through their business, grow it profitably and live a lifestyle of joy, abundance, and freedom. If this is not happening, they need to look at a new way of doing business.

This chapter highlights the *holy grail* of a successful 21st century small business. A new approach has been ushered in for small business owners. One that successfully grows their business more quickly and with less effort, while living a more healthy, balanced lifestyle. Demographic changes and cultural trends are causing them to approach hiring and decision-making differently. Small business owners are using a more holistic approach. These changes offer the small business owner more optimal solutions to their business challenges. They also provide more employee engagement and a better work culture. This supports and retains high performance employees more successfully.

Learn what the small business owner needs to know to create increased productivity, longevity, and profitability.

PERFORMANCE PILLAR 2: PEOPLE

Chapter 3:

It's All Management 101
by Clive Extence

We are all students. Or, we better be. We should be constantly learning. That is how I approached managing others, improving productivity, reducing scrap, and of course, facilitating classes for working adults. When I began teaching the adult learner, I understood and utilized the KISS principle (Keep it Simple Stupid). Now, that's not politically correct anymore – but you get it.

Reading this chapter, you will note these principles are distilled from 30 years of management and teaching experience. They are simple, readily understood, and hopefully, self-evident. The trick is to use them. Getting things done through others is "All Management 101". I ask, beg, and plead for you to get off your anatomy and use them.

Chapter 4:

Five Ways to Bring Compassion Into Your Organization
by Susan McCuistion

Think you don't have to worry about Diversity & Inclusion (D&I) because you're a small business? Think again! D&I isn't just for big companies – small businesses need it, too!

Navigating the complexities of D&I can be daunting. It's easy to be afraid of saying or doing the wrong thing, but avoiding it isn't a solution.

Businesses often "do diversity" because it's the "right" thing. The truth is, it's the only thing. When we look at diversity broadly – the influences, experiences, and education that create our unique perspectives in the world – it becomes obvious that diversity is a part of every interaction we have. From employees to customers to suppliers, you can't escape it, so you need to know how to best leverage it in your day-to-day business.

In this chapter, you will:

- Learn the basic history and terms around D&I
- Find out why D&I is important to your small business; and
- Create a link to a better way to "do" D&I – through compassion

Plus, you'll get a simple method for building more compassion into *your* business. Don't let diversity issues sideline you. Start embedding compassion in your business today!

PERFORMANCE PILLAR 3: PRODUCTIVITY

Chapter 5:

Spotlighting Yourself as an Undeniable Expert in Your Industry
by Becky Norwood

In this chapter, you will learn why smart business owners and entrepreneurs are choosing to include authoring a book as part of their marketing arsenal. Sharing their expertise in the pages of a book is a valuable "foot in the door" tool for business growth. The book establishes credibility as they showcase their knowledge of the subject they know best.

Authors often find that their book opens the door to speaking on stages, being interviewed on tv, radio, media, and podcasts. All of which can lead to joint ventures, as well as collaboration with other experts. It expands the business owners' reach to a global audience as they embrace the power of our digital age that offers self-publishing as a viable option for massive exposure.

Chapter 6:

Business is Addicted to Busyness, Not Success:
Improving Upon Decades of Failure
by Maggie Mongan

This chapter addresses one of the epic failures impacting Small Businesses in the first quarter of the 21st century – being addicted to busyness. The primary challenge Small Business Owners face is continuously getting snagged by the busyness trap.

Today's Small Business Owners are pulled in many directions. There is confusion identifying what requires attention versus what is a distraction. Throughout this chapter, we will expose how the *Small Business Owners Busyness Trap* is impeding success. We will do this by:

- Understanding how to become more Productive
- Learning how to work with *The Law of Diminishing Returns*
- Discovering the benefits of Productive Breaks
- Busting the Time Management Myth
- Recognizing how Distractions Kill Success; and
- Exploring if Technology Supports Success

Small Business Owners are the backbone of the economy. Studying and applying productivity is no longer a luxury. There is no need to struggle. Mastering these best practices is fundamental to moving beyond maximizing success to optimizing it. Continuous self-management is essential to winning big in 21st century small business. It's your future – choose wisely!

PERFORMANCE PILLAR 4: PEACEFULNESS

Chapter 7:

Discovering Your Business's True North
by Mike Raber

As small business owners and entrepreneurs, there are many different reasons why we are in business. The questions I ask, "What is your business's true north? Why did you decide to build a business? If you decided to sell your business tomorrow, what would it be worth?"

Join me as I discuss 6 simple (and often over-looked) lessons I learned as a seventh grader, which ultimately empowered me to successfully build multiple businesses over my career. What was the greatest lesson I learned? Business people who applied these key lessons were able to make choices in life – choices nonpractitioners weren't capable of making.

Over the years, I have continued to study many successful business owners and entrepreneurs who built both traditional and non-traditional businesses. I have found the secret to their success really came down to a few key points. Businesses come and go. The great ones grow into amazing companies and many disappear into the passages of time. In the end, it's often the business owners who follow these 6 simple concepts which leave their mark and blaze a path for others to follow. I invite you to continue our discussion by reading this chapter.

Chapter 8:

Are You Willing to be Successful?
by Susan White

Small business owners want to be successful. That's a given. This chapter explores a variety of definitions and perspectives of both success and willingness through the eyes of four practicing experts. It also visits the ways in which success demands a lot more than simple desire and concludes that it is a deeply personal definition that each of us create for ourselves. It debunks the myth that money equals success.

Additionally, it has us begin to explore our individual meaning-making systems of success and what we think we may have understood about it. Further, it determines how personal characteristics and core values contribute to success, as well as reviewing other common notions of success.

We learn that success is forever expanding and contracting, and is not a final destination. Finally, we begin to discover ways that we may already have created success and may not have even begun to identify it for ourselves.

UNDERSTANDING OUR CHAPTER LAYOUT:

Introduction to the Chapters' Brilliant Practicing Expert™
As the Founder & Creator of Brilliant Breakthroughs for the Small Business Owner book series, podcast, and mobile app, Maggie will introduce you to each chapter's author. She shares what makes the author unique via their skills and capabilities. Additionally, you will learn why the chapter's topic, through the lens of the author, matters to your business's performance.

Chapter Writing
Chapters are filled with tenured wisdom, proven tips, and experiences relevant to Small Business Owners (SBOs). We encourage you to learn and experiment to find your winning formula.

Chapter Glossary
All Brilliant Practicing Experts™ have terms they use in a particular fashion. Each chapter has a glossary to clarify what the author means as they impart their wisdom.

Author Biography Page
Each author wants you to become familiar with them. Included is a headshot, brief author description, and an invitation to connect with them further.

Business Page
Each author's business is represented with an informative page for you to become more familiar with the author's business. It contains a brief business description, and links for you to connect on their website and their social media accounts.

ADDITIONAL RESOURCES:

Book Purchases
This book is sold through Amazon.com and personally through each of the authors. For bulk orders, please contact Maggie Mongan at *https://www.brilliantbreakthroughs.com/contact-us/*.

To learn more about the authors, please go to:
https://www.brilliantbreakthroughs.com/small-business-owner-book-series/authors/
Here, you can meet all the authors online. Each Author's Page contains information about them and their business, as well as podcast interviews, videos, and social media links.

We also invite you to engage with us via our mobile app: BrilliantBizBook
Here, you will find similar content to the Author's Page as well as: new podcasts, blogs, events, new products and offerings, tips, tricks, and wisdom-sharings. You have us on demand in the palm of your hand once you access our mobile app!

Enjoy these fresh perspectives, meeting some Brilliant Practicing Experts™, and shining brightly!

PERFORMANCE PILLAR 1

PROFITABILITY

Brilliant Breakthroughs for the Small Business Owner

Allow Me to Introduce Brilliant Practicing Expert™
Kelly E. Andrew, by Maggie Mongan

I had the fortune of meeting Kelly through a mutual friend. I asked our mutual friend, "Who is the best Marketing and Online Relationship Building professional you know?" Within minutes, I was introduced to Kelly with only 3 words in the returned message: "She's the one." Great endorsement!

As I've come to know Kelly more, I agree! I haven't met a more conscientious marketer. Kelly's skills and capabilities in her specialty are exceptional. Kelly's expertise has allowed her the opportunity to align herself and her team with some of the best industry leaders.

When Kelly was writing her chapter's draft, she sent me 3 different versions. Each was exceptional. The knowledge shared was great. Yet, Kelly expressed she wasn't satisfied because she wasn't providing you with enough of what you need to up your game. We brainstormed how to share her wisdom with you in a different format and she went back to work. The outcome of Kelly's integrity and exquisite attention to quality is in this chapter.

Kelly is a strategist who is focused on the best possible outcome for her clients and community. Kelly is a change agent with beautiful visions. She has big goals for how to practically improve living and business in the 21st century.

The Inbound Pipeline to Success
by Kelly E. Andrew

If you haven't already implemented a strategic internet marketing plan, you've positioned yourself behind your competition. Marketing to your customers online is essential to your business's financial success. My intent in this chapter is to help introduce you to a practical, measurable internet marketing strategy to help you build a stronger, more sustainable business.

The Future Value of Your Business Depends on Internet Marketing

Max Palzewicz, CPA, and Financial Coach at ActionCOACH Business Coaching-Southeast Wisconsin explains that when it's time to place a value on your business, one major component in the calculation is **confidence in your business's future cash flow**. A key confidence indicator is a healthy and sustainable internet marketing and sales pipeline. "If you can demonstrate that you've got consistent conversion rates for impressions, appointments, and customers, it inspires a lot more confidence in your potential future growth, and that you have a plan to execute it well" (personal communications, June 27, 2018). If the time comes to sell your business, you'll show more value and be able to start negotiations at a higher price if you have data to illustrate a consistent internet marketing and sales pipeline.

Follow The Platinum Rule

Welcome to *Inbound Marketing*, a strategic, relationship-based approach to internet marketing that uses data to prove its success. *Inbound* is the opposite of traditional marketing, which forces itself upon consumers. It is no longer acceptable to bombard your target audience with TV, radio, or print ads and expect them to respond to your demands for attention.

Not only are these old marketing tactics ineffective and cost-prohibitive, but based on current consumer behavior, they're actually damaging.

Remember The Golden Rule, "Thou shalt do unto others as you'd have done unto you"? Today, smart marketers have embraced The Platinum Rule: "Thou shalt do unto others as they'd have done unto themselves." In his book, *The Art of People*, Dave Kerpen states, "The Golden Rule, as great as it is, has limitations, since all people and all situations are different. When you follow the Platinum Rule, however, you can be sure you're actually doing what the other person wants done, and assure yourself a better outcome" (Kerpen, 2016, p. 96). **Inbound** requires us to consider how consumers want to be treated, and tailor our marketing tactics to them.

Inbound Marketers Measure Success

Inbound allows you to quantify your marketing efforts and gauge success easily. There are hundreds of measurable tactics which support **Inbound**, including:

- Blogging
- Social media posts
- Pay Per Click (PPC)
- Search Engine Optimization (SEO)
- Offers
- Calls-to-action
- Landing pages
- Email newsletters
- Drip campaigns
- Segmented mailing lists/personalization
- Marketing automation
- Videos

- Podcasting
- Webinars

When it comes to testing and measuring your *Inbound* strategy, Jackie Steinmetz, CEO of Accelity Marketing says, "Make sure you hold yourself and your team accountable to results. It's not a Mad Men world anymore – marketing today is results-oriented and you have numbers to back up every initiative and to make smart decisions" (personal communications, June 12, 2018).

Strategy vs. Tactics

The marketing automation software, Hubspot's 2017 "State of Inbound" Report states: "If a company is slow to capture a new mode of communication, it might as well stop the business" (An, 2017, p. 46). Today, many business owners feel pressure to engage in internet marketing, but, instead of developing a strategy, they dive into one or more tactics, expecting results. Start planning your *Inbound* strategy by taking a look at the sales funnel:

Figure 3.

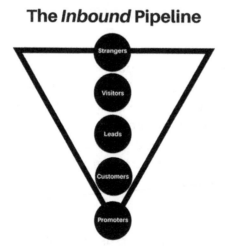

Source: Courtesy of Filament Communication

INBOUND STRATEGY #1: ATTRACT STRANGERS

Who are Strangers? Every consumer in the world falls into this category, before they become aware of your business.

How do they behave? 21st Century consumers are researching their purchases online. Strangers are one click away from finding you online every second of every day. "On average, Google processes more than 40,000 searches every second (3.5 billion searches per day)!" (Forbes.com, How Much Data Do We Create Every Day?, para. 2). Hubspot's 2017 "State of Inbound" Report states, "Salespeople acknowledge that buyers nowadays are more independent, and often bypass the salesperson completely. Gone are the days of the salesperson being the gatekeeper for information" (An, 2017, p. 56). This means you must position your website in a way which allows your target audience to find it on their own.

Tactics: There are countless tactics to support this step in the process, including SEO, PPC, social media, and blogging.

Important Metrics: This is a great time to look at where you rank for specific keywords, as well as your overall organic search ranking. The reach of social media posts, as well as the volume of visitors to your blog, are also good metrics to track.

Conversion: Your goal is simple: move strangers down the sales funnel to become visitors to your website. A more advanced conversion strategy would be to develop an ideal customer profile before employing any tactics. Focus on getting your website in front of people who fit the specific characteristics of your ideal customer. By customizing your tactics to engage only strangers who fit your profile, you'll see better conversion rates all the way down the sales funnel.

Practical Application:
1. Understand where you rank in organic search today, so you can employ tactics to make your business more visible

online. Establish expertise, authority, and trust with Google through your chosen tactics.

2. Get very specific about your ideal customer; go beyond age, sex, and location demographics to define them. Identify online behaviors and preferences, and remember The Platinum Rule!

3. Research keywords to identify what's being searched in relationship to your business; implement a keyword strategy.

CAUTION! Don't fall for vanity metrics. Let's say you've decided to use social media as a tactic to convert Strangers to Visitors. In this case, it doesn't matter if you have 50,000 Facebook followers if none of them engage with your content. Choose a more informative metric to track. What percentage of your monthly website traffic comes from Facebook? This statistic would indicate the effectiveness of your Facebook tactics month after month.

INBOUND STRATEGY #2: CONVERT VISITORS

Who are Visitors? Anyone who lands on your website, no matter how they found you, and no matter what page they enter on is a visitor.

How they behave: Visitors are on your site for one reason only – to find the information they're searching for. They can be fickle. (Have you been tracking your bounce rate? Isn't it incredible how many people find your site, but spend only a few seconds there?) In order for visitors to build trust with you, you've got to give them what they're searching for. If visitors can't find what they're looking for (ie: you've got it buried on a page which can only be accessed through two other pages), they will quickly bounce from your site.

Tactics: At this point, you'll need a mechanism to gather information from visitors on your website. This is where landing pages, forms, and calls-to-action, make an appearance in your plan.

Important Metrics: The volume of visitors who make it to your website is important to track; the more visitors, the larger the likelihood of conversion. Other metrics to help you understand your visitors' needs better include time-on-site, bounce rate, and number of pages visited.

Conversion: Website visitors become leads when they voluntarily give you some information about themselves. Collecting an email address is a great place to start.

Practical Application:
1. Know your baseline. If you haven't already installed Google Analytics on your site, do it today!
2. Start tracking where the conversion from Stranger to Visitor is happening. Google Analytics will show you where Visitors are coming from (ie: organic traffic, referral traffic, social media referrals, and direct traffic). Then, you can adjust your tactics accordingly.
3. Consider your site structure. How are your visitors experiencing your site, and how can you make it easier for them to find what they're searching for?

CAUTION! Visitors will not convert to leads if they aren't inspired to take your relationship to the next level. This is where your brand personality takes the driver's seat. Take it from Amira Alvarez, owner of Quantum Leap Coaching: "When it comes to marketing online, it's okay to be you. A lot of people are afraid to make a mistake, so they don't put themselves out there. This leads to very bland content. Go for it! Take a chance. Grow" (personal communications, June 11, 2018).

INBOUND STRATEGY #3: CLOSE LEADS

Who are Leads? Anyone who voluntarily gives you information about themself becomes a lead.

How they behave: Leads are interested in building trust so they can make an educated decision whether or not to purchase your goods; however, don't take this as your opportunity for the hard sell. Today's consumers demand this stage in the sales cycle be completed on their own terms.

Tactics: By now, your visitors have identified you as a possible solution to their problem. It's your turn to give them more information. Infographics, eBooks, quizzes, and product demonstrations are great tactics to educate your leads, and get them to share more information about themselves.

Important Metrics: A valuable statistic at this point in the sales process is the percentage of visitors converted to leads on the website. This is also a good place to think about implementing lead scoring for Marketing Qualified Leads (MQL) and Sales Qualified Leads (SQL).

Conversion: Your lead converts to a customer when they make their first purchase.

Practical Application:
1. Create valuable gated content. You'll engage your website visitors, and inspire them to give you information about themselves in return for the content you're offering.
2. Continue to gather information about your leads throughout their time in this stage of the funnel. The more visits they make to your website, the more opportunities you have to ask more questions (through forms), analyze their behavior, and respond accordingly.

CAUTION! You'll need to have a clear understanding of the term "lead" to hold your sales and marketing teams accountable. There's a big difference between someone who gives their first name and email address in order to download an eBook, and someone who completes a 20-question form giving a substantial amount of information in order to schedule a consultation. Discuss the criteria to identify MQL's and SQL's with your team.

INBOUND STRATEGY #4: DELIGHT CUSTOMERS

Who are Customers? People who've purchased from you at least once are customers.

How they behave: The customer's behavior can depend a lot on you! If they receive excellent service, and love your product, they're likely to become a repeat customer, and even move on to the next phase of the sales funnel. But, if they're not wowed, they'll likely disappear, never to be heard from again. Worse, if they have a negative experience of some sort, they'll blast you online.

Tactics: Asking for feedback is a key tactic in this phase. By caring about what your customers have to say, you engage them, and they're more likely to tell others how great you are. Feedback can come in many forms, but a survey delivered in an email is a great place to start.

Important Metrics: While you might already track how many customers you have and your revenue each month, there are a few other important metrics, which can help you project future profitability. What is your average dollar amount per sale? How many times does the average customer purchase from you? If you can identify the lifetime value of a new customer, you'll be able to set more realistic revenue goals for your *Inbound* Marketing Strategy.

Conversion: Customers become promoters when they start taking it upon themselves to tell your story and grow your business. They become part of your sales force.

Practical Application:
1. Ask lots of questions. Whether through an email, survey, or on a social network, your customers will become more engaged when you ask for their opinions.
2. Think of ways to surprise and delight your customers.

Following up to make sure they're completely satisfied with their purchase or offering them a special deal are great ways to go above and beyond.

CAUTION! Don't let the fear of a bad review stop you from implementing an *Inbound* strategy. Yes, the negative review will sting, but you'll be hurting your business far more if strangers aren't able to find you online.

INBOUND STRATEGY #5: DEVELOP PROMOTERS

Who are Promoters? Promoters are customers who become your best salespeople.

How they behave: Promoters take it upon themselves to shout your praises from the rooftops. They make it their mission to get their friends and family to use your product because they love it so much. They talk about you on their social media channels. They refer people to your business regularly. They love you, and they want others to love you, too.

Tactics: Engage with your promoters. Love on them. Interact with them on social media. Send them special offers via email. Acknowledge them as an integral part of your business.

Important Metrics: It's in this phase when you can really start to predict the future of your company. Tracking how many times a customer purchased from you and what their average purchase dollar value is will inform your entire *Inbound* strategy.

Conversion: Despite this being the final stage of the sales funnel, your goal is to convert the behaviors of promoters into new visitors and leads at the top of the funnel.

Inbound Next Steps

What should you take away from this chapter? Now is the time to start **Inbound** Marketing. In 2001, Greg Bernhardt founded PhysicsForums.com, an online science community which has grown to over 40,000 members today. He stresses the urgency of internet marketing to small business owners: "The effect of **Inbound** is cumulative. Ten years down the line, you'll have the kind of history where you can be the industry leader, but it's not going to happen overnight. Get started now" (personal communications, June 7, 2018). By implementing the **Inbound** Marketing Strategy, you'll build a sustainable internet marketing and sales pipeline and increase the future value of your business. Start today!

The Inbound Pipeline to Success
Glossary:

Blog: a regularly updated page on your website which features "posts" or articles.

Bounce Rate: the percentage of visitors to your website who leave the site after visiting only one page.

Call-to-Action: a mechanism used to inspire a website visitor to take action; typically a call-to-action is linked to a form that collects data about the visitor.

Content: online media like blogs, video, social media posts, eBooks, etc.

Conversion: the point at which a person moves from one phase of the sales funnel to the next.

Direct traffic: website visitors who reach your site by typing the URL directly into their Internet browser.

Drip campaign: a series of marketing emails sent in succession; this process is often automated.

Gated content: content that lives on a website, but is not available to a visitor without first filling out and submitting a form.

Impressions: the number of people who see a piece of your content.

Keyword: a word or words that are searched to help find specific content on the Internet.

Landing Page: a web page created specifically to support a marketing tactic and measure results.

Lead Scoring: giving value to a lead based on it meeting specific, measurable criteria.

Marketing and Sales Pipeline: the stages which a person goes through to become a customer; the amount of people in the pipeline determines the likelihood of a sale.

Marketing automation: technology that allows marketing tasks (like emailing) to be automated.

Marketing Qualified Leads (MQL): a lead which has been identified as more likely to purchase than other leads, based on pre-determined criteria.

Number of pages visited: how many different pages a visitor views on your website.

Offer: a piece of gated content used to collect information from website visitors or leads.

Organic search: the results shown to you by a search engine (not paid ads).

Organic traffic: website visitors who reach your website through a search engine.

Ranking: what order your website will be found in on search engines.

Referral traffic: website visitors who reach your website by clicking a link on another website.

Sales Qualified Leads (SQL): a lead which has been vetted by marketing criteria and has been identified as more likely to purchase, based on pre-determined criteria, sending it to the sales team.

Search Engine Optimization (SEO): multiple tactics used to increase a website's ranking in organic search.

Target Audience: people who match a specific criteria which identifies them as likely to purchase your product.

Time on site: how long a visitor stays on your website.

Meet Brilliant Practicing Expert™ Kelly E. Andrew:

Owner, Chief Ideas Officer, Filament Communication

In 2013, after a decade in the non-profit sector, Kelly E. Andrew founded Filament Communication. Her mission, to help independent businesses grow, inspired her to hone her internet marketing skills and build a passionate, growth-minded team of marketers.

Kelly believes that strong local economies depend on the success of independent businesses. Filament Communication helps those businesses shine online.

KELLY'S SPECIAL INVITATION FOR YOU:

To see if your business is ready to implement Inbound Marketing, visit: **https://www.filamentwi.com/brilliant-biz-book**

Business: Filament Communication

Filament Communication was established to support and grow Independent businesses through Internet marketing. While the Internet is changing every day, the Filament team makes it a priority to stay in front of trends and best practices, so its customers don't have to. By identifying and evaluating valuable Internet marketing metrics, Filament Communication implements strategic, sustainable tactics for its customers.

Filament offers brand, website, and SEO audits, strategic marketing plan development, Hubspot CRM and marketing automation implementation, SEO, content development and publishing, and analytic reporting and assessment. By taking a thorough, consistent, and sustainable approach to Internet marketing, Filament positions its customers for growth and future profitability.

Website: https://filamentwi.com

Connect with Kelly on these social accounts:
Facebook: facebook.com/filamentwi
Instagram: @filamentwi
LinkedIn: linkedin.com/company/filament-communication
Twitter: @filamentwi

Download Mobile App: BrilliantBizBook from your App Store.
It contains everything related to this Book Series and its Authors.

Brilliant Breakthroughs for the Small Business Owner

Allow Me to Introduce Brilliant Practicing Expert™ Nancy Clarimont Carr by Maggie Mongan

I specifically remember where I was sitting in my office the first time Nancy and I had a conversation – 3+ years ago! Considering how many people I speak with through any given year, it's odd how I can recall our first conversation years later. Perhaps, I should share *why* I recall.

Nancy was filled with joy. I could hear her smile beaming through the phone! She exuded confidence, without being arrogant. She was well-balanced. Over time, I've learned Nancy is consistent and a go-getter. When you read her chapter, you will notice this as well.

Nancy will share with you how to apply a fresh perspective to increase your profits. Even though many highly successful business owners have utilized this strategy and technique, and science has validated it as factual, it still isn't a common business practice.

NOTE: This chapter's topic could easily be placed in the fourth Performance Pillar; however, with its direct impact on profitability, we felt it would provide a greater fresh perspective if placed here.

Reading books about success that were written 100 years ago, will introduce you to similar wisdom-sharings and techniques. Today, you'll read a journey of how it's applied in this century. When you complete Nancy's chapter, you will have the opportunity to apply the same competitive advantage many of the high achievers utilize to succeed.

Higher Consciousness Creates Higher Profitability
by Nancy Clairmont Carr

How would your life change if your business grew faster, easier, and more profitably?

The methods to create a thriving, profitable business in the 21st century have changed: from unending work, a lack mentality, and profit at all costs to that of creating higher consciousness, an abundance mentality, and creating a win-win for all involved.

Many people, including me, grew up with the belief that, "To succeed, you can't rest until the work is done, and the work is never done." Not only is this false, but it can kill you. It just about killed me.

Growing up in an entrepreneurial family created my rock-solid work ethic. After 19 years of "unending work," I realized I had to change careers and my mindset or I wouldn't live to see my children grow up. I began my entrepreneurial path and decided to create new beliefs, paradigms, and a new approach to work.

Through study, new disciplines, and the use of energy work, I experienced consistent high performance with increased profitability, made possible by developing a higher consciousness. It is important that business owners understand what I call the new success metrics. Persistent long hours and no self-care program will increase burnout and employee healthcare costs and reduce performance and profitability. Success now implies support for *sustained energy for consistent high performance.*

Why should you adopt these new metrics as a business owner or key contributor in your organization? As you develop for yourself and create a supportive environment for WBH (whole body health: physical, mental, emotional, and spiritual), your work productivity and profitability will flourish.

There is a growing trend for business leadership to be defined as, "creating the conditions for yourself and your team to show up as fully human and the best version of yourselves to maximize your positive impact" states Rosie Ward, Salveo Partners (personal communications, June 12, 2018). Leaders in various industries are incorporating the new success metrics to thrive in the new economy.

- Arianna Huffington created sleep pods at her company and has written 2 books on the importance of sleep (*https://www.architecturaldigest.com/story/thrive-nap-room-coco-mat-arianna-huffington* para. 1-2).

- Dr. Mark Hyman, Medical Director at Cleveland Clinic's Center for Functional Medicine states, "The most elusive aspect of success is well-being, which encompasses physical, mental, emotional, and spiritual wealth. Money and power results too often from a sacrifice of the self, and the abandonment of simple principles of self-care" (*http://drhyman.com/blog/2013/06/03/the-third-metric-the-two-steps-to-solving-our-real-energy-crisis/* para. 2).

- Vishen Lakhiani, holistic transformation expert, supports, "self-awareness, connectedness and spiritual fitness to optimize potential for the individual and all of humanity" (*https://www.youtube.com/watch?v=tddzKkTzFUA&feature=youtu.be* Self Transcendence).

- According to Dr. Norm Shealy, neurosurgeon and holistic physician, energy medicine is the future of health (Shealy, 2010, front cover).

- Brendon Burchard proves that high performers are more energized mentally, emotionally, and physically than their peers (Burchard, 2017 p. 17).

- Deepak Chopra, MD, expert in mind/body medicine, states:

- Your mind, your body and your consciousness—which is your spirit—and your social interactions, your personal relationships, your environment, how you deal with the environment, and your biology are all inextricably woven into a single process ... By influencing one, you influence everything (***https://en.wikipedia.org/wiki/Deepak_Chopra***, para. 25).

The new metrics for high-performance output define how business and life will change.

These are the new 21st century workplace expectations:

- **Increased Productivity -** Technological efficiencies alone won't increase productivity. Companies require leadership enforcing healthier lifestyles. According to Roger Drummer, formulator at Herbworks.com, "The big mistake many small business owners make is not preparing for stress. Stress drops you into fight or flight, and intuition brings you into your upper brain. A morning practice of prayer, meditation/energy work, and proper nutrition opens up those energy centers, sets the energy for the day and affects every single thing a person does" (personal communications, June 6, 2018).

  Individuals who implement regular WBH programs can offset stress more effectively and bring more creativity and problem-solving ability to their work. This allows a person to access their intuition to receive more efficient and effortless solutions. "All creativity and vision are the result of intuition" states Dr. Norm Shealy (Shealy, 2010, p. 13).

- **High-Performance Longevity -** Long-term high performers want more. Being in alignment with the purpose of the organization, experiencing personal growth and contribution, and an ability to have a meaningful life outside of work is the new *holy grail* of work. Small business owners able to provide this to their employees helps offset a "VUCA (Volatile, Uncertain, Complex and Ambiguous) environment, where business disruption is the norm" states Rosie Ward (personal communications, June 12, 2018).

- **Increased Profitability** - Business owners and key contributors who have developed higher consciousness, are aligned with WBH energy, and engage their employees with work important to them will create higher profitability for their organizations.

Talent expert Dr. Mia Mulrennan, Rave-Worthy.com, offers a questionnaire for vetting customer service personnel and suggests these ideas for small businesses in hiring and working with high performers:

1. "Understand the qualities of people you do and don't want in your company.
2. Make sure the candidate is in alignment with your purpose and has clear expectations.
3. Use both assessment data and your intuition/feel about them" (personal communications, June 14, 2018).

What role does self-care play in creating WBH and contributing to business growth?

"What used to be considered unpreventable or irreversible health challenges are no longer viewed as such. It has been scientifically proven that we have influence over 95% of our well-being," shares Dr. Deepak Chopra. "We can prevent and reverse chronic conditions if caught in time and managed" (Chopra, January 2018).

This new approach requires us to no longer depend on others for optimal well-being. We are now personally responsible for our self-care. "Almost each and every one of us has the power and ability to heal ourselves through informed choices and a healthy lifestyle," concludes Dr. Robyn Benson. "In our own personal choices day-to-day ... self-care is going to ... not just transform your life, but all the people around you" (***http://robynbenson.***

*com/wp-content/uploads/2017/08/Module01_02_Body_Text.
pdf* p. VII).

Incorporating WBH practices including healthy eating, physical movement, hydration, relaxation, and mindset practices such as energy healing and meditation into our lives impacts our performance. Roger Drummer concludes, "Having a higher consciousness and being in great health makes you feel more alive. That is what people are looking for" (personal communications, June 6, 2018). We now have tools, experts, products, and support systems to help us achieve WBH. We can create a high-performance lifestyle.

I help small business owners reach higher consciousness as efficiently and effortlessly as possible. To achieve this, they need to decide this is important to them and worth the changes required.

The first change is to establish a new paradigm. Change can be difficult with unsupportive beliefs; therefore, it is important to know if their belief system can support the new outcome desired. If not, new beliefs need to be developed to drive their thought processes, habits, and actions for a new result.

Fortunately, new industries have been built around neuroscience, neuroplasticity, and neuroregeneration over the last 25 years. Science has proven we can change our brains and thought patterns. We no longer have to live with non-serving beliefs and programs. We can now control the expression of our DNA through lifestyle choices.

Bruce Lipton, Ph.D., discovered the molecular pathway through which thoughts affect every cell. He also proved genes express themselves based on environment, a science called epigenetics. He states, "We are not victims of our genes, but masters of our fates, able to create lives overflowing with peace, happiness and love" (Lipton, 2005, introduction, para. 1). This information proves we are 100% responsible for controlling our reality.

I discovered these concepts 20 years ago in my search for a new mindset. When I learned that everything is energy and how to use it, my life changed. I was a prolific personal development student using books, coaches, seminars, etc. It wasn't until I started experiencing energy healing and then became an energy practitioner; however, that I could permanently create thought pattern changes.

One of the tools everyone has is access to their intuition. Can using intuition optimize decision making? The data you have may have served you well so far. It becomes irrelevant, however, in this rapidly-changing environment. Using intuition for problem solving and decision making is required for finding optimal solutions.

According to Roger Drummer, "The information received from higher intuition comes through energy centers in the brain" (personal communications, June 6, 2018). Using intuition is more powerful than depending on our brain, which searches for past solutions that may not be optimal. Sonia Choquette states, "Intuition comes directly from one's Higher Self or Spirit and is subtle energy that connects us with the highest level and most current information from the quantum field to live our most empowered life" (***https://www.youtube.com/watch?v=jiB8WtnA4Ic***).

Intuition can be received through all of our senses: knowing, feeling, visions in dreams or while awake, hearing voices, and noticing smells. Using your intuition consistently will develop it more deeply. "Intuition is different than messages from your ego." according to Maureen Higgins, energy practitioner, "There is no effort or resistance when working with intuition, unlike messages from your brain" (personal communications, June 20, 2018).

Maureen Higgins states, "Working on yourself is the key to

success, because what you are attracts what you bring in. Any limiting beliefs you carry can interfere by blocking your energy field from attracting what you want" (personal communications, June 20, 2018). What she describes is what I experienced and is the reason I made major belief and thought-pattern changes in my life. I used energy-healing protocols to create these changes. As I developed WBH, accessed my intuition, released non-supportive beliefs and patterns, and increased my level of consciousness, I started manifesting more effortlessly and quickly in all areas.

Maureen Higgins shares:

> "The sciences are proving that everything has a vibration: words, thoughts, feelings. Through scanning and measuring the brain before and after a seven-week meditation experiment in beginners, Dr. Davidson from University of Madison found that meditation activated the happiness and well-being centers of the brain, and this produced more creativity" (personal communications, June 20, 2018).

Marcia Wieder states, "We could absolutely show and measure that happy people made happy employees and happy employees produce better results" (***http://robynbenson.com/wp-content/uploads/2017/08/Module01_02_Body_Text.pdf*** p. 5).

Bashar states, "Match the frequency of the reality you want, and you cannot help but get that reality" (***https://quoteinvestigator.com/2012/05/16/everything-energy/*** para. 18). We now have the tools to get us to the frequency or consciousness level we desire.

The most effective way to access intuition and increase consciousness is to learn to surrender. Surrendering is asking for and trusting you will receive solutions through your intuition. Surrendering provides the optimal solution in optimal timing. With consistent practice, you learn to trust this process.

Setting clear intentions is also required to receive optimal guidance. To understand the importance of intention, it helps to see the relationship of intention, mechanism, and result. I+M=R, *where the relative importance of I to M is 100%*. I = 100%, M = 0, R=100%. This relationship emphasizes that you don't have to know the specific "how" or "M" to get the intended result. There are infinite mechanisms that work when you accurately state and believe the intention. Surrendering will get you the optimal "M." The concept of surrender is difficult to accept because ego wants to be in control. It takes a strong desire for optimized results to be successful in learning to surrender.

Doing the work to develop higher consciousness yields many desirable outcomes. You:

- Become more authentic, trusting of self and others, non-judgmental of self and others
- More easily manifest intentions, access intuition and creativity, connect with others, develop new neuropathways, accept and create change, problem-solve, develop higher-level thinking, recognize opportunity
- Change paradigms from divisiveness to unity consciousness, lack to abundance, competition to cooperation, external validation to internal, living with limiting beliefs to optimizing your gifts, living out of balance to becoming aligned in WBH.

Developing higher consciousness provides considerable benefit to the small business owner.

The following are strategies you can incorporate to increase higher consciousness:

- Align your energy fields through creating WBH
- Reduce stress through mindfulness, breath work, movement, nutrition

- Incorporate energy medicine products containing nature's energies: essential oils, magnetic energy, negative ions, far-infrared technology, plant-based food
- Change your beliefs using energy protocols
- Remove the impact of trauma through energy healing
- Release negative ancestral, collective lifetime influences through energy clearing

Not knowing how to start the change process shouldn't keep the small business owner from implementing higher consciousness work. Knowing there are strategies and practitioners to help is what is important. Think of higher consciousness work as removing an energetic straightjacket, one that doesn't allow you to live your purpose or manifest a desired lifestyle.

Working with an energy practitioner to get unstuck, change a belief, and create new paradigms will maximize results and is the most effective and efficient change strategy. An expert energy practitioner will help you transform your paradigms and give you strategies to move forward independently.

My life was positively transformed by working with an energy practitioner and then becoming one. My business and profitability grew exponentially as well, while working less. Doing higher consciousness work to optimize any one area will positively affect all areas of your life. This is consistent with my clients' experiences also.

One client represents a typical outcome by implementing higher consciousness work. This client manages assets as a wealth manager that creates $1.5 million of revenue and was attracting clients with $500K assets or less. The intention was to attract new clients with assets of $1 million or more. By helping this client with belief changes, clearing negative energy, creating WBH, and replacing weekend work with self-care, my client attracted two significant new clients whose assets matched the top 10% of the prior year client's asset level. This client is now on track to increase total revenue by 20%.

Here are some questions small business owners should ask to decide the value of developing a higher consciousness as a strategy to create higher profitability:

Am I:

1. At the WBH level of sustained high performance?
2. Expressing my purpose through my business?
3. Accessing intuition for optimal guidance?
4. Growing my business quickly, profitably, and with less effort?

If the answer to any of the above is, "No," I encourage a decision for change, and that you consider the benefits of working with an expert energy practitioner.

Small business owners who want to increase profitability with the new success metrics must create a higher consciousness. It will help them receive optimal guidance; increase productivity and profitability while serving at the highest level; and shine their light on humanity through their purpose-driven work.

Higher Consciousness Creates Higher Profitability
Glossary:

Abundance Mentality: Empowerment-based mindset in which a person believes there are enough resources and successes to share with others.

Authentic: Real, true, of undisputed origin, genuine.

Chronic Condition: Health condition or disease that is persistent or long lasting in its effects.

Collective Lifetime Influences: Concept that all energetic beings are consciously connected; that collective energy influences our energy fields both positively and negatively.

Connectedness: Feeling of belonging to or having affinity with a particular person or group, to the degree that a person feels supported in life.

Consciousness: Quality or state of being aware, especially of something within oneself.

Energy Healing/Work: Holistic practice that activates the body's subtle energy systems to remove blocks to heal the mind, body, or spirit, allowing forward movement towards one's purpose.

Energy Healing Protocols: Written or verbal processes used in energy healing.

Energy Medicine: Natural and holistic approaches used for healing.

Epigenetics: Study of biological mechanisms that switch genes on and off; genes expressing themselves differently based on environmental influence.

External Validation: Getting approval from people outside oneself vs. getting approval from within oneself.

Far-Infrared Technology: Products and technology that incorporate or are based on the sun's energy.

Higher Consciousness: The consciousness of a higher Self; transcending reality and the mind's normal preoccupation with the past and the future; awakening to the unlimited nature of being; elevated awareness of spiritual essence.

High Performance Lifestyle: A lifestyle where whole body health (WBH) is created, allowing a consistent, high-level performance in all areas of life.

Holistic Physician: Physician who uses natural healing methods in addition to traditional western methods of drugs and surgery to treat patients.

Holistic Transformation: Change or improvement based on engagement in daily practices that organize body and mind towards well-being.

Holy Grail: Something that is being earnestly pursued or sought after that represents the highest value of its kind.

Intention: What one intends to accomplish or attain; what one has in mind to do or bring about.

Intuition: Ability to understand something immediately without the need for conscious reasoning.

Lack/Scarcity Mentality: Fear-based mindset in which a person believes there are not enough resources for all involved; a win/lose attitude where, when someone wins, someone else must lose.

Magnetic Technology: Products and technology that incorporate or are based on earth's energy.

Manifest: Bring about, show, exhibit, or demonstrate that which is intended.

Mechanisms: Strategies and techniques that serve to create something.

Mindfulness: Mental state achieved by focusing one's awareness on the present moment while calmly acknowledging and accepting one's feelings, thoughts, and bodily sensations.

Mindset: Established set of attitudes; a fixed mental attitude or disposition that predetermines a person's feelings and responses to and interpretations of situations.

Negative Ions: Products and technology that incorporate or are based on air's energy.

Neuropathways: Pathways connecting one part of the nervous system to another. These pathways are changed through energy healing to create new beliefs, actions, and results.

New Success Metrics: New ways of conducting business that drive productivity and profitability including high-performance longevity, WBH, employees aligned with the purpose of the organization, experiencing personal growth and contribution through work, and work hours that allow meaningful nonwork time.

Paradigms: Mental model, example, or template based on a certain set of beliefs and experiences.

Self-Care: Human regulatory function supporting any area of the body, mind, and spirit which is under individual control, deliberate, and self-initiated.

Sleep Pods: Areas in a work environment where employees can rest privately for a period of time.

Spiritual Fitness: Taking care of your spirit or soul or that which gives meaning and purpose in life to maintain its strength.

Stress: State of mental, emotional, physical, or spiritual strain or tension resulting from adverse interference which creates blocks or difficulties for the flow of energy, resulting in healing challenges.

Sustained Energy: Combination of mental, physical, emotional, and spiritual energy maintained at a high level over time.

Sustained High Performance: A consistent high level of quality and productive output over time using certain practices that can be replicated across all situations.

Unity Consciousness: Consciousness or spiritual level that recognizes all of humanity is connected and operates from the principal of love.

Upper Brain: Part of the brain containing the prefrontal cortex which contains all of the centers that receive and interpret sensory information, analyze information, reason, and experience emotions. Also called Higher Brain.

VUCA: Military term describing the environment in which it operates and the need to be ready for constant change: "Volatile, Uncertain, Complex, Ambiguous."

Vibration/Frequency: Level of consciousness; everything in the universe is made up of energy vibrating at different frequencies at the quantum level.

Well-Being: State of our mental, emotional, physical, and spiritual energy fields.

WBH: Whole Body Health; Simultaneous optimized mental, emotional, physical, and spiritual energy fields.

Meet Brilliant Practicing Expert™ Nancy Clairmont Carr:

Transformation Expert / Impact Coach /
Energy Practitioner / Speaker

Nancy Clairmont Carr empowers individuals to create the business and lifestyle they desire. After experiencing corporate business leadership and entrepreneurial success, she excels at helping business owners attain joy, abundance, and freedom.

Nancy works with conscious individuals, creating permanent exponential shifts in mindset, practices, and results. A certified coach, energy practitioner, and speaker, Nancy proves that higher consciousness creates higher profitability, outcomes not possible through old success models.

NANCY'S SPECIAL INVITATION FOR YOU:

Book a complimentary introductory session with Nancy to experience the possibilities: **https://www.TheJoy-Effect.com**

Business: The Joy-Effect

The Joy-Effect was founded to help small business owners develop higher profitability through higher consciousness— outcomes not usually possible through old success models. Nancy's coaching expertise creates permanent shifts in mindset, practices, and results. Her MBA, corporate marketing leadership, and entrepreneurial ventures allow her to quickly pinpoint what is needed for small businesses to expand. She incorporates her 30 years of experience and mastery as an energy practitioner to coach business owners to achieve/create quantum shifts in their business quickly and with less effort. The results are a business and lifestyle that bring joy, abundance, and freedom.

Website: https://TheJoy-Effect.com

Connect with Nancy on these social accounts:
Instagram: @nclairmontcarr
LinkedIn: https://www.linkedin.com/in/nancyclairmontcarr/
Facebook: https://www.facebook.com/NancyClairmontCarr,LLC
Twitter: @nclairmontcarr

Download Mobile App: BrilliantBizBook from your App Store. It contains everything related to this Book Series and its Authors.

PERFORMANCE PILLAR 2

PEOPLE

Brilliant Breakthroughs for the Small Business Owner

Allow Me to Introduce Brilliant Practicing Expert™ Clive Extence, by Maggie Mongan

Over 10 years ago, I was in a Master of Management business program. A new professor named Clive Extence entered the classroom. He was a different professor – one with actual experience in the business sector.

Clive was, and is, an excellent teacher. Why? He intimately knows his expertise of business operations and leadership. He went beyond the textbooks and taught the nuances of people management and business operations. Ultimately, his stories were filled with battle wounds and victories, which helped us understand realistic situations and management experiences.

Clive has mentored me though my Master Thesis, an article I co-wrote and presented in Vienna, various aspects of business development, and the first book in this series. He's a treasure of wisdom and is eager to share with anyone who's interested in success.

Today, I'm honored to introduce *you* to Clive. Being retired, Clive's chapter is different from the others. He shares applicable *pockets of wisdom* on a myriad of topics. He designed his chapter as a quick *go-to-guide* for you when you find yourself in similar situations.

Regardless of your team's size or location (in-house or outsourced), your business's performance will improve as you apply these realistic Best Practices. These are Best Practices of managing small business owners. Peace of mind will be your added bonus.

It's ALL Management 101
by Clive Extence

What follows are some points I feel the need to share based on my 25 years experience in production management (Operations and Plant Management) and facilitating adults at the university level for 25 years.

Effective leadership can be facilitated through the simple concept of understanding three questions, and these are: What? So what? Now what? The "what", of course, is the current situation or problem. The "so what" is the severity or priority given to the problem. And the "now what" is the important, yet most often neglected - what action should we take?

Students have repeatedly expressed appreciation for class discussions of these issues. I believe the reader will intuit their value. My wish is for the reader to look upon these points as springboards to **action**. *Italics* will be used to reinforce some of these points.

"In my experience..."

Be careful when hearing and using this statement. Statistically, what follows is often biased. We are culturally conditioned to trust what follows because, after all, "experience is the best teacher" correct? I would gently remind working adult learners - they are not the entire universe of this knowledge, and just because it's happened to you, doesn't mean it's the norm.

Action: Listen for this statement (from yourself and others). Pause. Ask yourself, "is there a better way?" Take the time to do the research. You can be fairly certain someone else has encountered a similar problem, solved it, and written about it.

Trust the studies

Some individuals invariably discount theories found in texts because they didn't match their experience. Meta studies seemed to alleviate some of their concerns. I would remind them of their Statistics and Research Methodology classes and how professionals have vetted these studies over many years. Too many students want new information, but it is simply too comfortable to keep doing what they are used to.

Action: Catch yourself and others in this regard and *stop it*! If you encounter a problem, open up a book or three (preferably from credible sources such as *Harvard Business Review)*, to see what others have done in similar situations. Do not assume what worked in the past will work in the future.

Little things don't mean a lot; they mean EVERYTHING!

Of all these maxims, I feel this is one of the most powerful. I remember it from a past management seminar and I've seen it in application ever since. It's all about recognition. Say "thank you" or "I appreciate the extra hours you've put in" or... It can be a cup of coffee, a pizza lunch, a personal note, or a literal pat on the back (yes, I'm from that generation.)

Action: It does not have to be budget-busting. Pay for coffee. Treat the department to pizza. Give some extra time off. Write (handwritten) a note of thanks or appreciation. Do it often. *But tie it to the performance you want to reinforce.* Change it up so as to not cheapen the currency. *All* employees love to be appreciated. (Beware of absolutes.)

Sloppy, lazy, management

Think about it. Think about your past bosses. Think about your last week's decisions. Were those decisions well thought out? Were they researched? Did you or your past bosses discuss them with the appropriate parties? Was there a plan B or C? Was there follow up? Was there fundamental learning planned for? Did your boss push you - just enough, not overly-burdensome?

Believe me, I'm as guilty of this as the next manager. We tend to make quick decisions (again, culturally-conditioned). If you think about it, *many*, if not *most*, of your decisions don't have to be made on the spot.

Action: If you can, ask for time to research the request or problem or at least sleep on it. You might make a better decision. Or, you could simply continue to practice what I've termed, "sloppy, lazy, management." This comment was overused in my classes based on some of the evaluations I received. But, years later, students bring it up when we run into each other.

Never, ever, use absolutes

We *all* have a tendency (culturally- trained) to use hyperbole when we communicate. How often do you use terms such as *all, always, never, many*, etc.? Do you think this might detract from your credibility? "If I've said it once, I've said it a *thousand* times…!" The reader is urged to study research on natural human biases.

Action: Stop it!

Praise in public, punish in private

Again, this can be considered one of those "absolutes." It generally works and is most often considered correct and common sense. Not so. Let me tell you a story.

Many years ago, I was a new manager and I already believed in the power of praising good work. So, when one of our better operators was asked if she would help train newer operators, she said "yes." After doing a fantastic job with a number of new hires, I took advantage of a department meeting to praise her in front of her peers. Cool, huh? Not so. She looked at me, turned red, then turned white, and began to cry. This was a tough, union woman who wasn't afraid to give me lip. I had embarrassed her.

This taught me to know and understand my employees, and to ask ahead of time if they would be comfortable with this type of praise. As an aside, this happened to me once again with another operator who was even tougher on the floor, and me - a union steward. I thought I could make some inroads using "praise in public" with her. The end result was the same. Beware of absolutes. These concepts don't always work. Especially when you've practiced "sloppy, lazy, management, as I had."

Action: Prepare for public appreciation by involving the parties to see if everyone is comfortable with your action(s). Drop your ego. Use the "Platinum Rule" (Bennett, 2013), not the "Golden Rule." The Platinum Rule: "Do unto others as *they* would have you do unto them."

Prepare to say "yes"

How easy is it to say "no" when an employee asks for something - anything? It's the lead in to "sloppy, lazy, management." Let's use a common employee request for a day off next week as an example. How about saying instead, "let me see what I can do; I'll get back to you." And then GET BACK to them. I used to remind supervisors of this by asking, "What will you do when the employee calls in sick?" Invariably, the supervisor would respond: "Oh, I'd just do this..."

Action: I'd respond, "Then why don't you plan for that now and allow the request?" *In my experience, too often*, some employees would call in sick for the day they were denied vacation. Why not make it a win-win situation? You will be surprised how often you can do this without giving the shop away.

I hype...you discount! (Negotiation)

From professor Dr. Charles Dwyer of Wharton School of Business (1991), this phrase turned the light bulb on for me. When we negotiate as influencer(s), we have a tendency to overstate the value being offered (hype). The influencee has a tendency to discount the value being offered. We are moving apart before we get started.

Our past negative experiences have trained us to understand this. Influencers forget this logical, common-sense roadblock. Dr. Dwyer's quote has stayed with me all this time: "Never expect anyone to serve your values unless you give them adequate reason to do so."

Action: This means be prepared to offer more. It doesn't necessarily mean money! Find out what employees value and provide it if possible. See: "Little things don't mean a lot, they mean EVERYTHING!"

Deming... 80% of errors... management's fault

Talk about trusting the research. I remember this fact from my student days in university. It was always amusing looking for the surprised yet knowing looks on students' faces when this point came up for discussion. I would ask: "Who makes all those errors, produces all that rework?" Of course, "operator error" would come up. But what William Edwards Deming found in his years of research was that over 80% of the errors for which managers love to point their fingers at employees, stem from inadequate management (1982).

I would say, *in my experience*, it's more like 90%! I would ask the class: "Who wants to go in to work tomorrow and produce crap?" In over 25 years of asking that question, only two hands went up and I know one of them, at least, was being facetious.

Do you want to produce crap? Think about your errors. Think about their errors. What caused them? Perhaps sloppy, lazy management? Perhaps overworked, under-trained employees? How about rigid bureaucracy? Perhaps poor morale? How about pushing employees beyond their skill level, even if you meant well? Maybe time constraints... "We've got to get this job out by the weekend. I don't care how you do it, just do it!" Trust that employees want to do good work.

Action: Do *everything* you can to provide employees with the training, knowledge, support, tools and materials, and communication needed to do good work.

Drop the ego

This is another concept from Dr. Charles Dwyer of Wharton School of Business (1991). If you want to be a good manager, then drop the ego. Ask your employees for direct feedback if you need help. But, be ready for the good, bad, and ugly. Do not do it if you are not prepared to love them for their honesty.

Action: Once a quarter, ask your subordinates for honest feedback, such as: "What am I doing that I should keep doing?" "What am I doing that I should stop?" "What more do you need from me?"

Stop judging others

"We judge others by their last bad action. We judge ourselves by our best intentions." This is my paraphrase of a Steven Covey (2008) quote. It is another one of those quotes from my past that has helped me manage others.

How many times have you thought, "What the hell is wrong with him/her?" "Why would anybody do that?" I'd be willing to bet others have said that about you. Professor Dr. Charles Dwyer has a quote to put this in perspective: "Have you ever heard anyone say, 'hey, you know me, I'm basically irrational!'" People make decisions and take actions based on what is important to them.

Action: Find out what is important to your employees. Find out what your employees value. Work on providing that for them.

Be kind (Henry James)

My favorite all-around quote. And I paraphrase here - it stems from a walk the British author, Henry James (1843 - 1916), had with some of his nieces and nephews. They asked, generically, the secret to getting along in life. His answer was profound: James gave them this advice: "Three things in life are important: the first is to be kind, the second is to be kind, and the third is to be kind." Now, as a manager, find ways to follow that principle.

Action: Take, for example, the corporate death penalty - firing one of your employees. This can be relatively easy - if you practice sloppy, lazy, management. And if you've done proper due diligence (to be moral, legal, and thorough), you are making it easier on you and your company.

What about your employee? Have you planned for what happens to them next? Have you used or offered an Employee Assistance Program? By the time you've made the decision to terminate, it's usually best for both parties. Can you make this more of a win-win as opposed to a win-lose?

Get off your anatomy! (Action)

Nothing will change unless you change. I was reminded of myself while observing students looking around the class, thinking they're not the ones who need this information, it's their boss who does. I know this because I used to feel the same way. I informed them, if they didn't get off their anatomy, future students would be thinking the same thing, only they'd be thinking of you.

Action is what's needed. Do all these ideas work *all the time*? Of course not. Try, succeed. Try, fail. Find out why. Act!

My wish, in this chapter, is to provide thoughts for you to ponder and actions for you to take so future professors will not have working adults rolling their eyes in class thinking, "my boss is the one who should be here, not me." Be a more effective manager. Get off your anatomy!

Meet Brilliant Practicing Expert™ Clive Extence:

Clive has worked in service and manufacturing environments for over 30 years. His vocation was industrial management as an Operations manager and Plant manager. His love, joy, and avocation was facilitating adult learning for two universities and multiple colleges. His passion was in bringing real-life experience to the classroom.

He has been retired since 2002, living on a lovely Wisconsin lake, and enjoying his 11 grandchildren... and wife.

Maggie was a former student in a number of Clive's classes and she was kind enough to invite him to come back to work (on this book). Clive has a passion for passing along his unique management and education experience to team members who have an interest in improving their business and management skills.

CLIVE'S SPECIAL INVITATION FOR YOU:

Subordinate your ego for the greater good - to the team, department, business, or goal. Contact: **cextence@charter.net**

Brilliant Breakthroughs for the Small Business Owner

Allow Me to Introduce Brilliant Practicing Expert™ Susan McCuistion by Maggie Mongan

Have you ever had a moment when you meet a person and you feel like you were friends your whole life? This is how Susan and I met. It's odd and cool all in one. I'm grateful for the many things she's taught me and how I didn't know I was functioning from different diversity myths.

Susan amazes me because she 100% lives and believes what she teaches. Most importantly, how humanity hasn't progressed as much as we perceive we have. Ready for this? This isn't an opinion, Susan has scientific research to validate it.

I appreciate how much Susan authentically cares about how people make other people feel by what they say and do or what they don't say or do. She's a champion for helping us navigate through the myths and misperceptions which continues to separate us from accomplishing greatness.

Susan's fresh perspective is a newer conversation to the Small Business Sector. Whether you're aware of this or not, this topic significantly impacts YOUR Business's Performance. Every aspect of your business is people-related. After you read this chapter, you will know how to be more aware of this and apply this research to create better relationships with everyone involved in your business and life!

Five Ways to Bring Compassion into Your Organization
by Susan McCuistion

As a small business owner, if you think, "Diversity and inclusion doesn't apply to me. It's only for big businesses," you're wrong.

> "Because of their company size or the number of people they employ, [small business owners] might not believe D&I issues affect them, or that they can't really do a lot about them. Maybe they believe it's too costly or too big to invest in because it's beyond them. They may not see that they can do even small things – like a simple approach to enhancing their hiring practice – that can make a difference in their organizational culture" (Jane Hyun, personal communications, June 18, 2018).

Businesses and organizations often "do diversity" because it's the "right" thing. The truth is, it's the only thing. When we look at diversity broadly – the influences, experiences, and education that create our unique perspectives in the world – it becomes obvious diversity is a part of every interaction we have. It's how we see the world – and how we interpret what we are seeing. Not only do diversity and inclusion permeate every area of our lives, but both are essential to building a successful, thriving business.

Efforts around D&I have been stuck for years. How did we get to where we're at today?

Starting with the Civil Rights Act of 1964, which attempted to plant seeds for social, political, and economic equality for all, the United States has tried to create a more equal nation. But progress has not matched expectations. Consider, for example, that the Equal Pay Act has been in place in the United States since 1963, yet women still only earn about 82% of what men earn (***pewresearch.org***, 2018, The narrowing, but persistent, gender gap in pay, para. 1).

Meanwhile, in 2016, only 27.7% of working age people with a disability were employed (bls.gov, 2016, Economic News Release, para. 10), **while more than 68% strive to work** (kesslerfoundation. org, 2015 Kessler Foundation National Employment & Disability Survey: Overview, para. 6). Likewise, only 21 states and Washington DC prohibit discrimination based on sexual orientation and gender identity (HRC.org, 2018, State Maps of Laws & Policies, map legend).

Unique to small businesses is a concept known as "diversity debt." Diversity debt

> "originated in the tech startup world, but which is applicable for all types of companies. Typically, you have a few people who come up with an idea, and they sell it, and the company grows fast. As they grow, they start hiring people. Generally, they hire people who are just like them. From the time you have ten or more employees, you accumulate diversity debt if you are not hiring with diversity in mind. There are now investors and analysts who are looking at diversity debt as a liability on the books" (Cathy Gallagher-Louisy, personal communications, June 8, 2018).

WHAT IS DIVERSITY & INCLUSION, REALLY?

At its most basic level, diversity is difference.

Within business, there is no way to avoid diversity. The world's population is diverse, so the talent pool is diverse, so our businesses are diverse. Our communities are diverse, so our schools and our places of worship are diverse.

It's easy to be overwhelmed with the idea of diversity when we think about all the possible differences that exist among people, but not all of these differences matter. The fact that I might be wearing a blue shirt and you have on a white shirt doesn't matter. The fact that I identify as a cisgender woman, while someone I'm working with identifies as a gay man, might. It's these "differences that make a difference" that we need to pay attention to in our day-to-day work.

"Inclusion" is often a word that goes along with "diversity" in businesses and, as a result, the two terms are often conflated. They are two different things. Diversity just is. Inclusion requires connecting people in an environment of respect so that their knowledge and experience can be leveraged within the company. It requires attention and intention, because of historic and systemic issues in which not everyone has had equal opportunity or rights. Women, People of Color (POC), LGBT, those who are differently abled, and others have been systemically excluded from businesses and leadership because they don't look, act, or think like the majority population.

Adding to the confusion around D&I are the many myths embraced about it.

We fight fires around specific topics when we need to – like race or gender or ability. But we never really get to the root of the myths driving the misunderstanding of diversity initiatives at large. Myths like, "Diversity is all about *them*," and "Diversity is a win/ lose proposition."

These myths foster not inclusion, but exclusion. How can anyone "win" an us versus them battle –particularly when both "us" and "them" are needed to get the job done?

THE POWER OF THE HEART

HeartMath® Institute (www.heartmath.com) has been studying the power and intelligence of the human heart for over 25 years. They have found that the electrical field of the heart is 60 times greater than that of the brain (heartmath.org, 2010, The Energetic Heart Is Unfolding, para. #4), and the heart's electromagnetic field can be measured a few feet away from the body.

The implications for business and D&I are powerful. It's easy to accept, "We're all human." It takes no effort to agree with someone with a similar perspective. The differences, though, are another story. Those are what we judge as right or wrong, and it's in those judgments that we get caught up in conflict.

When we connect at the heart, those differences become less of an obstacle. We can begin to see differences as interesting, rather than threatening. We cultivate curiosity instead of creating conflict. We let compassion drive our organizations.

COMPASSION IS NOT AN EXCUSE

One of the questions I hear most is, "By saying compassion is the answer, aren't we just providing an excuse to ignore the bad stuff going on?" But that is not how compassion works.

Compassion does not excuse the historic and systemic injustices in society. In fact, compassion demands even more effort than the old, worn diversity path that hasn't worked for years, because it requires us to actually take time to understand how these injustices affect everyone *from their perspective.* Reaching this point is a step-by-step journey, calling for not only deep introspection, but also an ability to recognize injustices, understand different perspectives, and step in to another person's shoes in a respectful, curious, caring way.

In recognition of this, more and more leadership research is focusing on areas like authenticity, vulnerability, and mindfulness. There is a growing acknowledgement, both inside and outside of business, of the need to connect with different people and perspectives.

COMPASSION AS SCIENCE

Let's take a look at some proven science about the benefits of compassion.

- **Making heart connections is good for our own health.**

Research shows (huffingtonpost.com, 2012, The Science of Compassion, para. 5) social connectedness can result in longer life, faster recovery from disease, higher levels of happiness and well-being, and a greater sense of purpose and meaning. Lack of social connectedness results in vulnerability to disease and death above and beyond traditional risk factors such as smoking, obesity, and lack of physical activity (***academic.oup.com***, 2018, The Potential Public Health Relevance of Social Isolation and Loneliness: Prevalence, Epidemiology, and Risk Factors, para. 7).

- **We learn new ways to see the world.** Compassion helps us discover and explore new perspectives. We learn there is not just one "right" and one "wrong" way for every situation. Embracing different perspectives helps open our mind to different possibilities, and build our problem-solving skills. We learn that two answers can both be right at the same time.

- **We increase our empathy and understanding.** The more we understand about ourselves and others, the better we are at creating deeper, more meaningful relationships. We're able to connect with others on mental, emotional, and even spiritual levels. As we gain a better understanding of other peoples' situations, we are able to help them in more authentic ways.

This is all great news on a personal level, but what does it mean for business?

BENEFITS OF COMPASSION WITHIN BUSINESSES

First, compassion within businesses relieves stress and burnout (***ccare.stanford.edu***, 2013, Compassion and Business 2013: Panel 1 of 4, video). Stress at work not only affects our health, it can affect our work relationships and focus, too (smallbusiness.chron.com, 2018, How Stress Affects Your Work Performance, para. 1).

Researchers find both the giving and receiving of compassion in the workplace decreases depression and negative feelings – like irritability and aggression – and increases creativity, performance, and productivity. People miss less work due to illness, which also decreases health care expenses.

Second, compassion increases a sense of community.
Compassion deepens connections to the organization and to each other (***psychologytoday.com***, 2013, The Unexpected Benefits of Compassion for Business, para. 5). When we care about each other and the work we do, we build better relationships at work, which leads to more commitment to the workplace. The end result is lower turnover and higher productivity and engagement (hbr.org, 2015, Proof That Positive Work Cultures Are More Productive, para. 4 & 6).

Third, compassion leads to better financial results (*hbr.org*, 2013, The Rise of Compassionate Management (Finally), para. 7). By now, this should be obvious. We all know the results of compassion we've already talked about – fewer absences, lower healthcare costs, decreased turnover, and higher productivity – lead to better financial results.

BUILDING COMPASSION IN YOUR BUSINESS

Hopefully, you're convinced about the benefits of compassion on a personal and organizational level. Here are the top five things you can do to develop compassion and build appreciation for diversity within your business.

1. Be present
In any situation, awareness is always the first step. How do we see a situation? How might someone else see it differently?

Often, when we teach D&I, we focus on self-awareness. It's important for us to understand our own perspective of the world. But awareness within compassion goes beyond just self-awareness. It encompasses things like mindfulness and presence, too. How do you connect with others? Do you really hear what they have to say, or do you listen just to spout your own answers and opinions? How vigilant are you about curbing your own assumptions and biases?

In research done for the book, *The Mind of the Leader* (**hbr.org**, 2017, If You Aspire to Be a Great Leader, Be Present, para. 7 & 8), more than 1,000 leaders indicated a more mindful presence was the best strategy to engage people, create connections, and improve performance.

2. Ask questions

Having an open mind means a desire to learn and engage with others in new ways. It means challenging our own ideas and opinions, and choosing to be open to other approaches and perspectives.

Accepting a situation does not mean we *agree* with it. We can still have our ethical and moral stances. However, when we have an open mind, we aren't as quick to label behavior as "unethical" from merely our own perspective. Instead, we respect and acknowledge there are other ways of moving in the world that are just as nuanced and complex as our own, even if we don't fully understand them.

3. Let go of expectations

The most compassionate thing we can do is not to treat others like we want to be treated, but instead, treat them as *they* want to be treated. This means letting go of some things, such as: preconceived notions of ourselves and others; long-held beliefs or ways of doing things; a particular path that's no longer working. For diversity work in particular, it means letting go of colorblindness, gender blindness, or any other blindness that minimizes our differences.

To be more effective in our work, we need to allow room for

others to be different from us. We need to make way for other perspectives and ways of being.

Most importantly, we need to realize there is almost never just one right answer. Instead, there are many good answers to each problem.

4. Manage your emotions

Our emotions are our internal guidance system. They let us know when things are going along according to our beliefs and expectations, and when they are not.

Emotional Intelligence isn't just about understanding our own emotions. It plays a key role in building empathy and understanding for others as well. When we are emotionally intelligent, we can connect with others on a different level. We understand their smiles may not be authentic. We understand that tears of joy may have behind them tears of fear and inadequacy.

Here's one of the most important things to understand about our emotions: *We can't stop* our initial feelings about a situation, but we *can* choose two things: 1) how we react to the situation; and 2) whether we remain with that feeling or shift to something more helpful.

What's more, the mood of the leader is one of the biggest influences on the company's bottom line. Depressed, mean bosses create toxic organizations filled with negativity. Upbeat, inspirational leaders have positive employees who embrace and overcome tough challenges.

5. Withhold judgment

Finally, we need to withhold judgment regarding the differences we are facing. Nonjudgment is not easy, because our brains are wired to make judgments. Some of the judgments we make are necessary for our survival – like fleeing a burning house. However, many of our judgments in business come from our own biases, fears, and inexperience. We must make it a priority to withhold judgment in situations that are not life or death situations, even when it goes against every fiber of our being.

It's important to understand, "We all want to be respected," and still know there are differences in how we show respect.

It's important to believe, "We all want to be successful," and to remember we all define "success" differently.

It's important to recognize, "We are all human," yet, still grasp the historical and systemic challenges faced by different groups.

To realize the second half of these statements, we have to be willing to withhold judgment. We cannot know there are different ways to show respect and still demand respect in only one way. We cannot understand different definitions of success and require people to follow a specific path to succeed. Most importantly, we cannot grasp historic and systemic issues without managing our own biases about the role we may have in upholding those systems.

WE CANNOT IGNORE DIVERSITY

Diversity is our world's natural, default state, and it is the basis for small- and large-scale person-to-person interaction.

Understanding diversity through the lens of compassion helps us not only better understand our own perspective, but see things from other perspectives. When we develop compassion, we can affect change through understanding what others truly need *from their perspective – not what we think they need.*

Businesses that recognize this, plan for it, and engage with it will be prepared to not only meet the demands of the future, but also build stronger, more successful businesses today.

**Five Ways to Bring Compassion into Your Organization
Glossary:**

Barriers: Any block to equal treatment for a group of people. Some barriers may be historic – e.g., handed down through history, such as practices around segregation – and others may be systemic – e.g., built within the system, such as recruiting or interview practices that are intentionally or unintentionally built to exclude certain groups of people.

Cisgender: A person whose gender identity matches the sex they were assigned at birth.

Civil Rights Act of 1964: Landmark United States civil rights and labor law that outlawed discrimination based on race, color, religion, sex, or national origin.

Diversity: The influences, experiences, and education that create our unique perspectives in the world. Any of the differences that make up who we are, including but not limited to: gender, race/ethnicity, generation, sexual orientation, religion, ability, veteran status, where we grew up, family status, education, etc.

Diversity debt: When startup companies or small businesses do not take diversity & inclusion into account when hiring, they end up with a homogenous group of employees. Companies with diversity debt are less resilient in response to crises, have lower innovation, and create more toxic work environments.

Exclusion: Intentionally or unintentionally ignoring or mistreating a person or group of people based on their personal diversity characteristics.

Gender identity: One's sense of one's own gender, which may or may not correspond with the sex assigned at birth.

Inclusion: Connecting people in an environment of respect, regardless of their differences. Giving equal access and opportunity to all people and removing barriers for those groups who have been historically or systemically discriminated against.

LGBT: Acronym for the three sexual orientations and one gender identity of Lesbian, Gay, Bisexual, Transgender.

People of Color (POC): Any non-white group of people.

Sexual orientation: Describes how one's personal sexual identity aligns to the gender they are attracted to.

Meet Brilliant Practicing Expert™ Susan McCuistion:

President, daiOne, LLC

Susan McCuistion is a cultural practitioner and creator of Compassionate Diversity®, which integrates concepts from the fields of intercultural competence, emotional intelligence, leadership, neuroscience, and more into powerful tools for change.

Compassionate Diversity® uses three interrelated concepts – Comprehension, Connection, and Compassion – to help build empathy and create an action plan for addressing the historic and systemic issues that are part of our current world.

SUSAN'S SPECIAL INVITATION FOR YOU:

Compassionate Diversity® is grounded in seven principles. Learn more about these principles and get practical tips for building more compassion in your business by attending a free webinar. Sign up for the next session here:
https://www.susanmccuistion.com/p/registration-page

Business: daiOne, LLC

diaOne, LLC trains and supports with people and businesses to establish the foundation, build the tools, and develop the skills necessary to achieve measurable, effective, and lasting results through inclusive and values-based approaches.

When you understand how to fully connect with everyone in your business – from employees to customers to suppliers – you'll increase innovation, build influence, and boost sales.

Website: https://SusanMcCuistion.com

Connect with Susan on these social accounts:

LinkedIn: **Susan McCuistion**
Facebook: @SusanMcCuistion
Twitter: @SusanMcCuistion

**Download Mobile App: BrilliantBizBook from your App Store.
It contains everything related to this Book Series and its Authors.**

PERFORMANCE PILLAR 3

PRODUCTIVITY

Brilliant Breakthroughs for the Small Business Owner

Allow Me to Introduce Brilliant Practicing Expert™ Becky Norwood, by Maggie Mongan

Becky and I met at Brendon Burchard's High Performance Academy. We bumped into each other during the event and had great conversations about life, how we've served humanity, our goals, and how to consistently perform at high levels.

The bonus? We learned Becky is a 21st century Publisher. Her depth of the ever-dynamic publishing industry is point-blank amazing. I've spoken with many publishers and she is exceptional. Not only is she proven as a successful publisher, she also has strong experience in guiding Experts and Business Owners on how to utilize a book to boost their business.

Becky is a rare find in her industry. Not only does she share the reasons why you should do this, Becky's approach is contemporary and comprehensive. She has created a streamlined process for the non-sensical process of publishing. It, like her, is high quality and delivers desired outcomes of authors.

In this chapter, Becky will discuss the surprising benefits of publishing your expertise in a book. I will add, there's even more than she is sharing here, but it's a great start. Do yourself a favor and make sure you read this chapter. If writing a book isn't for you, you'll still learn how to better position your business in your marketplace.

Spotlighting Yourself as an Undeniable Expert in Your Industry
by Becky Norwood

As a business owner, an entrepreneur in your own right, how do you distinguish yourself as different from others that offer services, products, expertise, training, or coaching that is similar to what you offer? In this incredibly noisy digital world, our competition is just keystrokes away.

How do you keep the clients you have coming back to you again and again, and how do you cost-effectively attract new clients?

Have you let the world know that you are a noteworthy authority, with comprehensive solutions to the issue or problem they want to solve? Does your voice get lost in all the noise?

Do you know how to use storytelling in your marketing, to make potential clients sit up and take notice?

You are passionate; you have a viable product. Your coaching is stellar; your service is top-notch. How do you set yourself apart from your competition, once and for all?

No matter how big or small a business is, smart entrepreneurs, look for ways to increase revenue.

What are the alternatives?

- Create a new product
- Add new services
- Carry new products
- Raise your prices

While creating or carrying new products and services is a wise thing to have in your business arsenal, there comes the point that there is a cap to how much you create before you confuse your end-user, and wear yourself out. The same goes for raising prices. How much can you raise them before pricing yourself out of the market?

Maximizing and growing your revenue is about taking a good look at the tools that abound at our fingertips in this fantastic world of our digital age. Never before has there been so much available to us, often with a sizable price tag. The shiny object syndrome causes paralysis by analysis, robs the bank account, and overwhelms your spirit.

The question becomes, how do you expand your reach, creating new areas of revenue and serve a national or even an international market? How do you duplicate yourself, without working 24/7 and wearing yourself to a frazzle?

It is not entirely about marketing. It is about a different way of grabbing attention. It is about rising above the noise. We always hear about the value of social media and other forms of marketing. However, if you are using social media to drive potential clients to your website, how are you enticing them to stay, to buy, or to hire you for the knowledge, expertise, and authority in which you shine?

Today's potential clients want connection. They want a reason to stay. They need to "know, like, and trust," that you do indeed offer the real deal. Satisfy that, and often you have a returning client for years to come.

How do you do accomplish this?

One of the most powerful tools available today is a book. Not just any book. YOUR Book.

A **business book** is a tool that savvy business people are implementing as a smart marketing tool. Why? People have respect for authors. If someone has written a book on a topic that holds his or her interest, he or she must know something about the subject. A business book establishes you as the expert and is a valuable tool.

A book lets the world know you are a noteworty authority, someone they can go to for comprehensive authority. Written with careful attention to detail, combined with marketing strategies that will seve to establish your expertise, and serve as a tool for business growth.

A small privately-owned hardware store that had always been THE place to go for our local farming community was feeling the pinch, struggling to stay afloat. With the suburbs stretching to the smaller towns, and Lowes and Home Depot opening, it looked as if they might need to close their door. The solution? As they analyzed their consumer base, they noticed that aside from the old time farmers, they also had a younger set of the do-it-yourself type that was frequenting their store. So, they became a resource store, offering both classes, and short books with simple step-by-step instructions their clients could quickly thumb through so they could get their job done. They combined this with links to videos they'd created and put on YouTube, for the visual connection clients needed. Now they are doing well and have carved quite a niche for themselves with an unlimited supply of you fix-it classes and books.

By authoring a book, you can effectively either launch a business or notably grow an existing business, because you have become "the expert who wrote the book."

Your book will serve you by:

1. **Defining your Brand**: As with any business, an author will brand themselves across all marketing platforms, including social media, videos, website, and printed materials. An author will weave branding into the book and business with a theme that uniquely showcases storytelling with

the human touch, and therefore, credibility. It's your uniqueness that will cement your branding.

Karen Liz Albert, Social Media Expert/Strategist at Behind Your Curtain, LLC insists that, "The importance of an author creating a brand that is more representative of themselves vs. their book(s) is that it allows for them, as the author, to be looked at as the subject matter expert, with their book being a product that supports that position. It also opens up the possibility for the author to publish more books in the future. The social media sites that promote and brand the author should be considered the "umbrella" branding sites for which all future books can fall under" (email communication, September 4, 2018).

2. **Growing your platform and Establishing Your Expertise**: Publishing a book can help you connect with your audience, helping you become a personality instead of just a generic business. Writing a book shows your clients what you're about and the depth of your expertise. By consistency, you will grow your business, using your book as a valuable foot in the door tool.

3. **Generating Leads**: How will writing a book create leads? When you begin your journey to becoming an author, you will do your homework. What search terms do people use when looking for answers to the questions for which you are an authority? Incorporate those buzzwords as you craft your book's content. As potential clients search for answers or are in need of your product/service, your strategic marketing will help them find you. They're also more likely to buy from someone who is a published author. Because your book provides educational, useful content, the first person, your readers, will contact is you.

For example: I have wildly naturally curly hair. I have tried many salons, often unhappy with the lack of knowledge on how to cut and style hair of this nature. I'd go from the Little Orphan Annie look, to straightened hair that took a lot of time and effort to care for. Then I found a book written specifically for us curly-haired individuals and not only was their haircare advise superbly beneficial, but I was also able to locate hairdressers in my area trained in the techniques the author taught. Since then, I have been in love with my hair!

4. **Connecting you with Influencers:** Using a story of your past to interact with your audience, using your own vulnerability, bringing to light insecurities and fears, then infusing it with hope, by saying, "I was in your place too," allows you to connect with other influencers who faced the same or similar obstacles. Often, these key influencers know people who should know you.

5. **Establishing Credibility by Educating and Becoming a Resource:** The best way to market yourself is to educate. When you educate, you become a resource. When you become a resource, you build credibility. When you build credibility, you create loyalty. Loyalty will result in clients that "know, like, and trust" you and who look to you as the "go-to expert." As you build that respect, they will buy not just your book, but your product, service, coaching, and will attend your events. A book gives potential clients and customer's tangible proof as to how much you understand your field, proving his credibility and trustworthiness.

Sue Ferreira, Video Marketing Expert, Wisdom to Wealth Mastery explains that, "In today's noisy world, speaking and video are the most powerful marketing tools an author can use in conjunction with their books to establish credibility and become a trusted resource" (personal communication, September 7, 2018).

6. **Increase Your Ability to Attract Publicity to Your Book and Business:** The media, including TV, Radio, and Podcasters are regularly looking for new content and covering not only new book releases but also unique perspectives in all areas of expertise. Tying the topics of your books with current events is a powerful strategy to attract media coverage.

    Your book will reach a broader audience and, have the potential to reach new customers for your existing business once it gets picked up by the press. Jenn Foster of Elite Online Publishing shares, "Our client, Marilynn Barber, Author of "Dress Like You Mean Business," landed interviews with ABC news after publishing her book. It developed into a full television talk show series hosted by ABC, due to the exposure she gained because of her book" (personal communications, September 3, 2018).

7. **Speaking Opportunities:** Area trade organizations and professional groups are often interested in having authors speak at their events. Leveraging your content, sharing to a broader audience at speaking engagements bite-size pieces of your expertise. Establishing yourself as an author and speaker can be a remarkable source of revenue for you as an owner.

    Meina Dubetz, Author of "When Death Comes Knocking for Your Patients: A Guide for Nurses and Palliative Caregivers" was delighted to share, "Publishing my book has opened doors! Nursing schools and organizations for palliative caregivers are now using my book as a teaching tool for their students" (personal interview, August 28, 2018).

    For Example: A client we have is a speaker and coach. He was in a quandary when he came to us. Each time he booked a speaking engagement, planners would ask if he had a book. He also wanted to have something he could offer from the stage that would serve as a tool for attracting new clients. Since writing his book, both his speaking engagements and his client base have increased, and he has gone on to write both a second book, as well as accompanying courses.

8. **Attracting a Different Audience to Your Brand:** Your usual client base may be among the first to purchase your book, but often, because of the expanded reach your book brings you, your story reaches a broader audience of readers searching for specific content related to your niche. Once you've established yourself as a valuable resource to this new audience, there will be a natural interest from that new book customer to support your underlying business as well.

   Charmaine Hammond, CSP, MA, professional speaker, and top expert in collaboration and sponsorship states, "Being an author built my influence, credibility, reach, and recognition of my brand. My book launches and tours have included sponsorship by both local businesses and major corporations. This type of collaboration is a true win/win and a source of incredible exposure for both my book and my business" (personal interview, August 30, 2018).

9. **Building Up a Social Media Following:** The publicity that you create by getting people excited about a new book will be an opportunity to grow your social media following. Using a combination of your consistent and unique branding, use of video, and consistent messaging, you will build a new tribe of followers.

10. **Charging More**: The truth is that "celebrities" in any field get paid more. It's why exposure is so important. Getting yourself recognized as a thought leader in your industry

will increase your credibility. Your clients will pay more because they expect more from you.

Everett O'Keefe, International #1 Best Selling Author and Founder of Ignite Press, spoke about his own experience and that of one of his clients, "Since writing "The Way of Wealth" my client, Frank A. Leyes ChFC has tremendously increased his client base, what he charges for his services, and his opportunities to command the stage. As his publisher and author myself, my rates have tripled, and I have become a sought-after book publishing expert" (personal interview, August 31, 2018).

I like to use the story of the Chinese Bamboo tree to drive this point home. Like any plant, it requires sunshine, water, and good rich fertilized soil to grow. However, after providing all the proper conditions, there is never evidence of any growth at the end of the first year. The same for the second, third, and fourth years. Suddenly, in the fifth year, you see a small sprout bursting through the soil. Then, in six short weeks, the bamboo tree grows 80 feet!

How does this plant sustain this phenomenal growth? In the previous years, it was growing a powerful underground root system that would support its growth.

Strategically planning and implementing smart marketing that includes a book will result in business growth. Undoubtedly, it won't take the long five years that the Chinese Bamboo Tree took to grow, but providing all the right conditions for business growth, such as publishing a book, will lay the groundwork of a solid foundation. The book becomes a valuable tool in your business arsenal, and much like the roots of the giant Chinese bamboo tree, that tool will sustain you for years to come.

The reasons to write a book are many. It may be a passion project; you write about a cause for which you are passionate. You may decide to write a book to generate revenue and business growth, to build authority, to grow your network, or to share a story of triumph over adversity. It could even be a fictional story crafted to entertain.

Of course, there is more to becoming an author than what we have discussed in these few pages.

Spotlight Publishing™ is passionate about not just helping our clients publish a book. We work with our authors to cultivate and grow the results that can come from that book by teaching them smart marketing. Our authors begin their marketing the moment they put pen to paper, or, start tapping the keys of their keyboard.

Not sure where to start?

Tip # 1: Take an hour and brainstorm. Write your ideas. Make a mind map of all the ideas you have for the content of your book. Do not filter any idea that comes to mind at this point. Get all of your thoughts on paper. I've had clients who have used a blank wall and post it notes. Don't worry if it is messy, crazy, and seemingly insignificant. It is a fabulous starting point that will serve you well. It is a valuable way of visually organizing your ideas, and you will be surprised at what can come from this.

Tip # 2: Begin marketing in the very early stages of writing your book. Sound odd? It is not. Get your following engaged. Use social media, write a blog, send out an email and let your fans know how excited you are that you have started writing your book. Get them engaged, but posting about your progress as you move forward. Ask for feedback on the title and book cover. Ask trusted followers to read your manuscript and give feedback. Generating excitement will go a long way towards attracting a tribe of followers.

Get Seen. Get Heard. Get Sales.

In today's world, you have the advantage of a vast array of tools at your fingertips. That includes your book. That is how it's done!

Spotlighting Yourself as an Undeniable Expert in Your Industry Glossary:

Attract a Different Audience: Authors often gain exposure to uniquely different audiences that would never have known about them before publishing.

Attract Publicity: Because marketing includes press releases and book tours, authors often attract media interviews.

Author: An individual who has published a book.

Author Brand: Every author needs to brand themselves not only with the cover of their book but across all social media, printed promotional material, email correspondence and website so that they are easily recognized.

Become a Resource: An author becomes a "resource" due to both the content in the book and subsequent information that is shared while speaking, in videos, training, etc.

#1 Best Selling Author: Becoming a #1 Best Selling Author serves much the same purpose as a diploma or degree one attains with education.

Business Book: A business book, is a book written by a business owner or an entrepreneur to showcase their area of expertise.

Change Agents: Often, authors share stories of triumph over adversity or write about a cause that they are passionate about, thus becoming a force for change in our world.

Charge More: The added exposure that comes with publishing a book lends itself to being thought of as the "go-to expert," enabling them to charge more for their products and services.

Connect with Influencers: As speaking engagements and

networking opportunities arise, those you connect with, know others who could benefit from what you teach.

Credibility by Educating: Educating within the pages of a book establishes credibility and opens the door to empowering others even without our presence.

Digital Age: Digitally-based items such as cell phones, social media, podcasts, videos, automated email systems, self-publishing, and more, enables us to grow our business even globally.

Establish Expertise: Writing a book is a viable platform for becoming known as the expert on the subject matter taught in the pages of the book, thus establishing their expertise.

Generate Leads: An author wisely plans a book to include opportunities to connect, thus generating leads.

Grow Your Platform: A platform is your following, and your book is the tool to help you expand your reach and exposure to speaking and collaboration opportunities.

List Building: Incorporating automation tools to build a mailing list that enables an author to continue to "touch" those seeking more guidance and information and increases the potential of turning them into clients.

Speaking Opportunities: Every author that I have worked with has told me of unexpected speaking opportunities that arose due to someone discovering their book.

Smart Marketing: Publishing a book is quite simply a smart marketing decision!

Meet Brilliant Practicing Expert™ Becky Norwood:

Book Publishing Expert, #1 Bestselling Author, Speaker and Coach

A lifetime entrepreneur, Becky Norwood is now a book publishing expert, #1 Bestselling Author, Speaker and Coach whose passion for excellence shines through as she has worked her magic with over 50 authors. Bringing them to #1 bestselling status by implementing smart marketing practices has made publishing worth the time and effort for her clients.

Becky married her husband, Mark, 11 years ago, blending five adult kids, and now nine grandchildren. Camping and crafting are her chill-time favorites along with enjoying her growing family. She is currently the social chairperson for her local Soroptimist chapter.

BECKY'S SPECIAL INVITATION TO YOU:

Eight-part mini-series on "The Art of Powerfully Using Storytelling in Marketing."
https://www.spotlightonyourbusiness.com/storytelling

Business: Spotlight on Your Business | Spotlight Publishing

The inspiration for Spotlight on Your Business began with the sole purpose of working with business owners to implement smart marketing practices. Seeing many businesses stricken by the economy, Becky was inspired to learn best practices for marketing using technology that would not only simplify life for business owners who hired her but also keep them in front of their clients. After becoming proficient in cross-channel marketing, she also became a certified book publishing expert. Becoming an author is a remarkably powerful tool business owners can use to establish their expertise and catapult their business success. Becky has brought over 50 authors to #1 Bestselling, and her focus with each author is teaching them to treat their book as a business and educating them on simple, yet effective ways to keep both their book and their business in the spotlight.

Website: https://www.SpotlightOnYourBusiness.com

Connect with Becky on these social accounts:
LinkedIn: https://www.linkedin.com/in/beckybnorwood/
Facebook: https://www.facebook.com/Spotlightonyourbusiness/
Twitter: https://twitter.com/urbizspotlight
YouTube: http://bit.ly/2on5isc
Author Profile: amazon.com/author/beckynorwood

**Download Mobile App: BrilliantBizBook from your App Store.
It contains everything related to this Book Series and its Authors.**

Allow Me to Introduce Brilliant Practicing Expert™ Maggie Mongan, by Meg McNally*

I met Maggie over 11 years ago through an organization to which we both belonged. We had many things in common, least of which was a multitude of years in the *corporate* world. Even though the industries were different, we understood the demands – time, resources, and personnel – on our respective companies and on us!

When I was guided to explore a business for myself and move away from *corporate*, Maggie was guided to assist me and several others. She spoke a language I didn't understand – the small business owner language. Just like a recalcitrant student, I fussed that the translation of small business didn't match my *corporate* knowledge. Imagine my surprise when I started my business in a new geography and found myself right in the middle of other small business owners who understood and ran their businesses via Maggie's 4 Performance Pillars!

I was gifted the opportunity to work with Maggie. I am very grateful for that and the very special friendship that was formed. Maggie is a patient teacher while demanding you to bring forward the best you've got. She is tremendously insightful and will motivate you to learn, stretch, set goals, and achieve more than you think possible. She truly closes doors for those things that no longer serve you (and your business) while opening new windows. Whether you've worked in the *corporate* world or have been fortunate enough to always be a small business owner, Maggie has knowledge and gifts to share with you – so that you can find joy, profitability, productivity, and peace with your business.

*Meg McNally is the President of Bowheart Business Strategies

Business is Addicted to Busyness, Not Success:
Improving Upon Decades of Failure
by Maggie Mongan

In only seven years from when this book is published, the year will be 2025. Most likely humans, specifically Small Business Owners, still may not have broken their addiction to busyness.

Other than the Great Recession of 2008, this may be dubbed "The Epic Failure of Business" in the first quarter of the 21st century. This seems illogical with all the technology, tips, and techniques we have available to help improve productivity. Yet, between the ongoing research and conversations with Small Business Owners, the *busyness trap* appears to be a primary challenge.

You are about to go on a unique learning journey. If you choose, this chapter will provide you with significant insights regarding how your performance impacts your business's performance. We'll begin by clarifying foundational concepts of our topic before we dive into the different facets of busyness and success. Ready?

What's the Small Business Owner Busyness Trap?

It's the trap you get in when you're busy doing a multitude of things, but at the end of the day, you haven't accomplished what's necessary or you didn't move your business's performance forward as intended. It's similar to a merry-go-round. To start and sustain the momentum of the merry-go-round, it takes enormous energy and action. It can be spinning at a fast pace, but there isn't any traction – only a great deal of energy expended.

Small Business Owners (SBOs) can create their own busyness trap by not knowing what best serves their business, or by creating unfavorable habits, which impedes upon success. If this is you, we're going to help you understand how to improve your and your business's performance.

Small Business success in the 21st Century isn't patient. Small Businesses must become successful shortly after launching or it becomes increasingly difficult to be successful as time passes. Thus, the UN-Experts will give you endless lists of things to do to keep you in the busyness – with minimal return. But how could you know any differently from what they're telling you?

SBOs create and build their business to be successful for personal and/or professional reasons. Usually, they are interested in swiftly achieving their goals. Surprisingly, candid conversations reveal their average pace is much slower than anticipated. Why? They are hindered because their productivity isn't as vigorous as intended.

Defining & Understanding Productivity

Productivity is a word most of us think we can define, but don't even get close! According to BusinessDictionary.com, productivity is: "A measure of the efficiency of a person, machine, factory, system, etc., in converting inputs into useful outputs" (***http:// www.businessdictionary.com/definition/productivity.html***, para. 1). In other words, productivity is a mathematical formula to determine how effectively inputted resources are converted to outputs.

Common conversation doesn't properly use productivity. Usually, SBOs are referencing how *efficient* something is or isn't. Unless a person is specifically addressing the measurements of input and output in a formula, they are usually referencing efficiency instead of productivity. We will use BusinessDictionary.com, to better understand productivity, by defining efficiency and effectiveness.

Efficiency is defined as: "The comparison of what is actually produced or performed with what can be achieved with the same consumption of resources (Money, time, labor, etc.)" ***http://www. businessdictionary.com/definition/efficiency.html***, para. 1). A SBO practical application of this is: with the same amount of resources,

Person A may produce or perform better (be more efficient) than Person B.

Effectiveness is defined as: "The degree to which objectives are achieved and the extent to which targeted problems are solved" (*http://www.businessdictionary.com/definition/effectiveness. html*, para. 1). SBOs often use effectiveness as percentages of completing or achieving something.

Clearly, *efficient* and *effective* are cousins in the *family of productivity*, explaining why they're often incorrectly applied. Now knowing the definitions and differences of these terms, SBOs should begin to better address their business's performance needs.

Why is understanding this important? Your Business's Performance is determined by measuring and analyzing your productivity, efficiencies, and effectiveness. Once you have these metrics (numbers), you know what is and isn't performing well and can experiment with new actions to attain improved performance.

Small Business Owners Addicted to Busyness

Were you thinking I may have sent you on a scenic detour with all this productivity talk? Good news, I didn't.

For years, I've blogged about the threats busyness infuses into a business. Last year, I wrote in the #1 Bestseller: Brilliant Breakthroughs for the Small Business Owners (2017) about how we, as a society, are addicted to busyness. I briefly shared how busyness shows up for SBOs and how it's often confused for productivity.

Why does busyness occur? It's a powerfully unfavorable habit many SBOs acquire. Busyness damages progress. It prevents SBOs from making bold power moves to improve the business's performance. Busyness supports all action with minimal to no traction.

Busyness deteriorates impact and success until you are eroded. Once eroded, you play small and accept small wins as the norm instead of performing to your potential. Busyness is dangerous. It prevents you from achieving.

Have you noticed how people are wearing their busyness as a *Badge of Honor* these days? Don't fall into this trap. If you do, you might as well be saying, "I'm a reactionary and don't have any discipline to stick to a plan. I'll go where the winds will take me." As a customer, would you be inclined to give that business your money and trust them to make you a priority? No.

Let's shift and discuss how busyness is equally harmful to humans. If not stopped, busyness leads to burn-out. I've experienced burn-out. Burn-out hurts – you come to a screeching halt and can't function.

Busyness is a by-product of not living intentionally or purpose-driven. It demonstrates to others how you don't have priorities or boundaries. It validates you are undependable. Yikes!

TIP: What's the best solution to the busyness trap? Don't say, "I'm busy." It confuses people or may provide an unfavorable perception of who you are.

NOTE: Successful people aren't busy. Their time is intentionally scheduled to complete appropriate tasks to move performance needles in the right direction.

CAUTION: The Law of Diminishing Returns

There are concepts, scientifically proven, which are called Laws or Universal Laws. There is one relevant to busyness and success which is named: *The Law of Diminishing Returns*. This common economic theory describes "how at a certain point, increasing labor does not yield an equally increasing amount of productivity. In other words, when the amount of input increases over time, at

some point, the rate of output decreases for each unit of input"
(**_https://www.learning-theories.com/law-diminishing-returns._**
html, para. 1).

Many SBOs are consistent at unknowingly applying this Law
to their business day. Here's how it commonly appears: You're
working on a project and you're exhausted. Instead of taking
a break to revitalize yourself, you keep pushing through. There
comes a point, that no matter how many resources you put into it,
you aren't getting the return you should – it's diminishing.

Here's the reality check: this Law doesn't discriminate if you're
enjoying what you're doing or not. It's much easier to identify this
when you're working on something you don't like.

Having a great work ethic worked well for me when I was in
corporate America, but it actually created havoc for me as a SBO.
I didn't know when to quit. I felt like I was failing as a Business
Owner. This was confusing for me until I learned _The Law of
Diminishing Returns_.

This helped me realize it doesn't matter how hard I can "push"
myself – the efficiency and effectiveness won't be present. What
saved me? I created new habits. Over time, I learned these same
habits needed to be applied by most of my clients for them to
succeed too.

Productive Breaks Support Success

Continuously performing at high levels isn't natural for humans.
Machines, yes; humans, no. Is there value for you to extract from
all those high performance and high productivity conversations
and techniques? Yes!

High Performance and Continuous Improvement are constants in
the business world; however, it has gained some new momentum
again. Brendon Burchard's #1 Bestselling Book: "High Performance

Habits" is deeply anchored in research and reveals *The 6 Habits of High Performance*. It's a great read and even better if you apply Burchard's teachings of how discipline and balance are essential to improving one's performance.

For almost 10 years I've been blogging about this, and similar aspects, to help Business Leaders effectively and efficiently perform. Why? All SBOs want to spend less time working.

When focusing on improving your output, you must improve your input. The science of this is very simple. If you're a factory and want to create a greater output, you simply get more raw materials to put into the system. Then, you get more output. You already know this!

Yet, we are humans and our physiology requires so much more. Regardless of our willingness and dedication levels, all humans have mental, biological, and emotional *Laws of Diminishing Returns*. When we take breaks, we revitalize or regenerate our performance capabilities.

For over a decade, the research consistently tells us we perform better when we take breaks, eat lunch, and use our vacation time. Do we do it? No.

We need to honor being human and give ourselves what we need to better function. Lora Polowczuk, Chief Energy Officer of Priority Retreats states, "Proactive recovery allows you to slow down to be more effective" (personal communications, July 27, 2018). Get better at this and you will improve your success rate.

Myth buster: There is no such thing as time management!

We all have 24 hours/day to do what we do. We cannot manage time – it simply is. What we can do is manage our productivity within each 24-hour period.

Our challenge lies within self-management. As children, our thoughts and actions were continuously corrected. Wouldn't it be great if someone would correct you when you deviate from your plan for success? That person is you!

My clients always share how self-directing is magical. Achieving the results of personally set goals is exhilarating.

NOTE: The challenge is not knowing how to effectively: set goals, create strategies/plans, self-manage, and self-correct. A tenured coach, mentor, or guide who has accomplished what you seek is your best answer.

True experts can teach you new habits to assure that your mindset and actions are in alignment with your stated goals. They can teach you how to become more mindful of your gaps and how to improve them. Accountability to learn new habits is paramount for achievement. Without it, you will fall back into your old ineffective habits.

Distractions – The Silent Success Killer

One of the best ways to achieve business success is to simplify. I wrote a chapter on this in our first volume (2017 book) in this series. Simplifying works because it helps you "Keep the Main Thing the Main Thing" per Stephen R. Covey. It removes distractions.

Understanding workday interruptions is essential for improved self-management. In 2006, Dr. Gloria Mark was interviewed by Gallup. She revealed that when we're interrupted, it "takes 23 minutes and 15 seconds" to attain the same level of concentration we had prior to the interruption. Dr. Mark's research also revealed self or internal interruption accounts for 44% of all interruptions (*https://news.gallup.com/businessjournal/23146/too-many-interruptions-work.aspx*, paras. 17 and 23).

SBOs have endless distractions. Are you working to remove them? Can you outsource some of it to another person or automate a system for it to immediately handle what is slowing you down from what you really should be focusing on?

Is Technology Supporting Success?

My industry observations reveal this is where SBOs lose the battle. As a group, we haven't figured out how to move beyond creating busy to creating success.

We have plenty of tips and technology tools but effectively applying them isn't being accomplished. Business success rates are becoming more challenging because tech provides a myriad of tools and most SBOs believe they must use all of them OR they get so frustrated they don't use enough of them.

Tech, with all its capabilities is a SBO's best friend. The common tasks we can now automate and outsource are remarkable. The ability to conduct business anywhere and anytime is lightyears ahead of how we functioned 15-20 years ago.

I am an advocate of tech. Yet, I must ask: Have the tech geniuses let us down? Yes, they have. They've created some great things but haven't helped us learn how to utilize and master these tools. Instead, what I consistently witness is tech mastering SBOs. This needs to change.

I predict an ocean of potential when it comes to learning how to effectively and efficiently use tech to boost productivity. The tools are many. Some are great. Yet, most tech creators still haven't figured out how to integrate the human and the tech tool or application. I'm not talking about Artificial Intelligence, I'm referring to the step prior – us effectively using tech tools to support our lives, goals, and ambitions.

Too many apps are isolated, myopic, and aren't user-friendly. SBOs are drowning in the sea of productivity apps and tips. So why haven't we mastered this yet?

Decades ago, we were told we would have much more free time because of all the things the computer could do for us. After all, tech is an efficiency or productivity tool.

Do you find yourself relaxing more than you're working each day? I'm not. Each year, I'm finding it increasingly difficult to *not* get distracted by tech and getting sucked into the Busyness Trap.

Dave Rebro, a #1 Bestselling Author who's dubbed the "Tech Therapist", is a solution. He helps SBOs right where tech has left us stranded – at the intersection of productivity, technology, and victorious living and business. Rebro states, "Find tech to serve your purpose, the way you think and work, what you're trying to achieve. Frustration and overwhelm will revert you back into the busyness trap because there's no clarity to get you where you want to go" (personal communications, July 27, 2018).

Optimization, not maximization, is the key to success in the 21st century. Business Transformation and Human Potential Expert, Kerrie Hoffman of FocalPoint Business Coaching states, "Use technology wisely. Systematize the minutia ... elegantly automate the things that matter" (personal communications, September 4, 2018). We must consistently challenge ourselves to simplify our business's success.

Small Business Owners Productivity Boost: Choosing Wisely

You are the most valuable asset of your business. Your performance matters most to your business's success. You choose how you show up and what you accomplish. Choose wisely!

Avoiding the busyness trap is paramount for Small Business Success. Immediately remove yourself when you find you're in it. Don't worry, it happens to everyone.

Choose to eliminate busy work. Block time for all your activities and adhere to your plan. Outsource as much as possible.

Automate whatever you are repeatedly doing. Find tech which will best support your mission.

Study and apply best practices of the most successful. Secure a guide to help you develop and practice success. Most importantly, choose success!

Business is Addicted to Busyness, Not Success: Improving Upon Decades of Failure
Glossary:

Badge of Honor: Something we pride ourselves on.

Burn-out: When one is physically, mentally, emotionally, and spiritually exhausted.

Busyness Trap: Do many things, but not gaining the traction in the right things you need to be successful.

Distractions: Something that prevents you from concentrating on what you need to focus on.

Effectiveness: Officially defined in the chapter. The degree to which something is completed. Usually expressed as a percentage.

Efficiency: Officially defined in the chapter. Essentially a comparison of how things are produced with minimal resources.

Internal Interruptions: When we interrupt ourselves instead of something external interrupting us.

Interruptions: When someone or something temporarily stops you from focusing on your task.

Proactive Recovery: When you take a break to recover before you are depleted.

Productive Breaks: Restorative breaks, pauses, lunches, time outs, or vacations.

Productivity: Officially defined in the chapter. Measuring the efficiency of inputs to usefully produced outputs.

Self-correction: When you correct yourself to stay on task.

Self-directing: When you guide yourself and your activities.

Self-managing: When you control yourself.

The Law of Diminishing Returns: Officially defined in the chapter. Simplified: at a certain point, no matter how many resources you put into producing something – it doesn't increase more production.

Time Management: A myth. We can't control time. Each day has 24 hours – no more, no less.

UN-Experts: An expert usually of online marketing, but not an expert at whatever it is they're offering. They don't deliver sustainable results for their customers.

Meet Brilliant Practicing Expert™ Maggie Mongan:

Master Business Coach & Trainer | # 1 Bestselling Author
Conference Speaker | Small Business Success Influencer

Raised in rural Wisconsin, #1 Bestselling Business Author, Maggie Mongan approaches business like many local farmers – practically, proactively, and always looking "Forward". Her entrepreneurial journey began as a teenager. With over 30 years of leadership and management, Maggie serves Entrepreneurs and the Small Business Sector. She is a trusted guide, training clients on business's fresh perspectives to Simplify 21st century Small Business Success. Maggie is recognized as a Small Business Success Influencer.

MAGGIE'S SPECIAL INVITATION FOR YOU:

Learn more about YOUR Busyness & Productivity Levels in a short video series and receive a guide to keep you focusing on what matters most. Go to: **https://BrilliantBreakthroughs.com/ Busyness**

Business: Brilliant Breakthroughs, Inc.

Brilliant Breakthroughs, Inc. was established to help Small Business Owners learn how to optimize, not maximize, their leadership and business performance. Additionally, to provide the same competitive advantage corporate gets, but as a fraction of the cost.

Good news: there is a new way of conducting business! Maggie helps clients reverse failures and build simplified business models for success by implementing her proprietary framework of *The 4 Performance Pillars for Small Business*™ (profitability, people, productivity, and peace). Bottom line: Maggie swiftly helps Small Business Owners succeed by simplifying strategies and aligning actions to build their profitable and peaceful business.

Website: https://BrilliantBreakthroughs.com

Connect with Maggie on these social accounts:
LinkedIn: https://www.linkedin.com/in/MaggieMongan
Twitter: https://twitter.com/BrilliantBlogr
Facebook: https://www.facebook.com/BrilliantBreakthroughsInc/
YouTube: https://www.youtube.com/c/brilliantbreakthroughsinc
Author Profile: **https://amazon.com/author/maggiemongan**

**Download Mobile App: BrilliantBizBook from your App Store.
It contains everything related to this Book Series and its Authors.**

PERFORMANCE
PILLAR 4

PEACEFULNESS

Brilliant Breakthroughs for the Small Business Owner

Allow Me to Introduce Brilliant Practicing Expert™ Mike Raber, by Maggie Mongan

Even though Mike doesn't look like it, he is a non-conformist. From his earliest days, he marched to a different beat! Most people under-estimate Mike. Why? He's unique, but not a unicorn. Additionally, he's a quiet leader.

I met Mike over 3 years ago. I am revitalized every time I speak with him. Here's what makes Mike different: he is wicked smart, practical, and a visionary. His genius shines brightly. He deeply listens to learn what is genuinely important to you and then reminds you of it at the most opportune time.

Humor is a great asset when speaking of serious business. Mike's timing is exquisite to lift the stress.

Did I mention Mike's a great people connector? I've never seen a person care more about and do everything possible to support the right people to connect.

This chapter highlights a child's first entrepreneurial journey. It reveals how he found solutions to challenges and experimented until desired results were achieved. Additionally, the chapter continues with a wisdom-sharing of 6 Key Lessons, decades of research and unconventional techniques mixed with further experimenting to successfully sell a business. Demonstrating: sometimes, business is much easier than we make it!

Discovering Your Business's True North
by Mike Raber

As small business owners and entrepreneurs, there are many different reasons for why we are in business. The questions I invite you to explore are, "What is your business's true north? Why did you decide to build a business?"

Entrepreneurial Youth Experience

I have been an entrepreneur for as long as I can remember. The beginning of my seventh-grade year, my class decided to sell chocolate bars for a fundraiser. The student who sold the most chocolate bars would get recognition and a prize.

I made up my mind that I was going to be the winner. However, I knew it wasn't going to be easy. You see, I went to an inner-city school and lived in a very poor neighborhood. Many of my neighbors were lucky if they could put food on their table. So, to buy chocolate bars, no matter what the fundraiser was for, was a luxury many could not afford.

Many of my classmates thought selling candy bars was stupid. But the ones, who did want to sell them, went door to door on the same blocks I would have to. Talk about a saturated market. 20 kids selling candy bars on the same 6 blocks to people who couldn't afford them.

I knew if I was going to win, I would have to think outside of the box. So I went to the library and got a book on selling and another one on marketing. One chapter talked about the importance of identifying your target market. Another discussed identifying your competitive edge. Yet another explained the advantage of creating a strong value proposition. I thought they were great concepts; the question was, "How would I apply them to selling chocolate bars?"

I grabbed a pen, some paper and started writing down different ideas. This is what that seventh-grader came up with:

Concept #1: Identify my target market. Simple, people who like chocolate. That narrowed it down to just shy of 90% of the people in my neighborhood.

Concept #2: Identify my competitive edge. The chocolate bars I was selling were great tasting, high quality and the only way people could buy them was through a fundraiser.

Concept #3: Identify my value proposition. When people bought the chocolate bars from me, they would be supporting a good cause, through helping my school.

Ok, I was ready for business, or was I? Putting down my pen, I grabbed my box of Chocolate bars and headed out the door. After knocking on fourteen doors, eleven told me they didn't have any money, two already bought chocolate bars from another classmate who beat me to the door. And another was on a diet. What being on a diet had to do with buying chocolate bars from me, I will never understand. After all, didn't they have any friends?

All my aspirations of making it big in the chocolate bar business was quickly coming to an end. I needed a new plan. Something the other kids in my class wouldn't think of, or at least, wouldn't do.

Immediately, I re-examined the 3 concepts I had just learned; identify my target market, identify my competitive edge, and identify my value proposition. I needed to find a market which liked chocolate bars and *could afford to buy them*.

Next, I needed a market differential. I needed to find a market that wanted my product and didn't have other people selling to it. I remembered going to a park near Lake Michigan on Lake Drive. There were many large expensive homes up and down Lake Drive.

I explained my dilemma to a friend of my mom who lived near there. It turned out the kids who live in that neighborhood didn't go door to door. If they had a school fundraiser, their parents would bring the items being sold for the fundraiser into their offices for their co-workers to buy instead. Guess what I did? I packed up my chocolate bars and headed for Lake Drive.

I wanted to look like I was from the neighborhood. Even though it was only 45 degrees outside, I decided not to wear a jacket. And to top it off, during the day, mostly older women were tending to their grandchildren while at home. I was sure they could appreciate my efforts of trying to help my school.

I got off the bus and walked around the corner and just stood there in awe. You could fit two if not three of the houses on my block in any one of the houses on Lake Drive.

After taking a large gulp, I attempted to knock on my first door. An older lady came to the door. I explained that I was selling chocolate bars for my school. Seeing I wasn't wearing a coat, she asked if I was warm enough and if I wanted some hot chocolate. I told her, "That would be great." After a short time, I finished my hot chocolate and sold her 10 chocolate bars.

The next house bought five more and on it went until all the chocolate bars were gone. The following weekend, I replenished my stock and returned to Lake Drive where I once again sold all the chocolate bars. I ended up selling five times as many chocolate bars as anyone else and won the contest.

My seventh-grade year ended up being a pivotal point in my journey towards my becoming an entrepreneur. I learned many things about business and the great benefits which can come from having a business, whether it's small or large. However, the greatest lesson I learned: people who had successful businesses were able to make choices in life which those who didn't have businesses couldn't.

I spent the rest of my seventh-grade year designing a prototype for an organization that would support, empower, and help entrepreneurs and small business owners to build a successful business. And have been working on it event since. In order to continually fine tune the process, I have spent the last 30 years building different businesses, while coaching and helping small business owners take their businesses to the next level.

Lessons learned along the way

Year's back, while sitting in a calculus class, I wrote a business plan for a limousine company. Then I set out to bring it to life. It turned out to be an amazing learning opportunity. Not only did I learn a lot through the process of building, running, and eventually, selling the business. But I was able to spend a majority of my time around different CEO's, CFO's and other successful business owners.

Reflecting to when I first started learning about business as a seventh-grader, trying to sell the most chocolate bars through now, there are a few key concepts that helped mold the business person I am today. They are as follows:

When starting a business, continually "Build a financial asset not just a job" (Dean Fliss, president of Global View Capital Advisors, personal communications, July 11, 2018). People will start a business or even buy an existing business thinking they are going into business for themselves. Realistically, what they have done is just created their own job. FYI: I would argue the true value of a business is what it will produce without you (working) in it.

I suggest you follow what I refer to as the five-year plan. First, create a point of valuation of what your business *should* be worth in five years. Then focus on the activities needed to create value within your business. At the end of five years, you now have three choices: (a) sell the business and do something else, (b) keep the business and hire someone else to run the business while you go and do something else, (c) or continue running the business yourself – extending the date out another five years. If you do option (c), ask yourself: what will your business look like and be valued at in another five years? It's this method which makes it possible for someone to own and run many successful businesses, while earning a lot of money, and living a great life.

In the book, *Start with Why* (2009), Simon Sinek talks about the importance of truly understanding your why. If your why is strong enough, you can overcome any obstacle. Do you truly know why you're in business? Does your why extend beyond yourself? Do the people within your business and your customers also understand your why? Do they also share in that why? Most importantly, do they have a vested interest in the success of your business (pp. 133-153).

This even held true when I was a twelve-year-old selling chocolate bars for my school. My why was twofold: I wanted to support my class's fundraiser *and* I wanted to win the contest. The houses I went to also shared in my *why*, and wanted to help support my class's fundraiser. I'm sure some of the houses bought chocolate bars just so I could go home before I caught cold – since I didn't have a jacket and it was getting colder as the sun started to go down. Who knew my discomfort would become a great selling point? Clearly, we shared a *why*.

Another powerful lesson I learned along the way, from the recording, *The Strangest Secret (1950)*, Earl Nightingale states "Watch what everyone else does – do the opposite. The majority is always wrong." When it comes to business, don't follow the masses. Rather, find a non-traditional approach to your business's focus and how you build it.

A great example is when I ran my limousine company, I had new vehicles, professional chauffeurs, and endless advertising. I was positioned at the head of the pack, when it came to the limousine companies in the area. This was great. However, I wanted my customers and clients to have a reason to call me – even if they didn't have a need for a limousine service.

I wanted them to look at me as a true resource. I wanted to capture a piece of their heart. Over time, I gained the respect and trust of my clients as not only a great limousine company, but also an important resource for their colleagues, friends and family. Each week, this provided a constant flow of many new referrals.

Just like with the chocolate bars, I knew I needed to think outside of the box. I was already doing what everyone else was doing. I had already built great relationships with my clients. Through continuous networking, I knew many different types of business owners. I needed to find a new way to differentiate my business.

Next? I developed a referral directory of all the business owners and professionals I worked with. Then I started to brand myself as a high-end concierge, like what you would find in a five-star hotel. I told my clients that when they needed the services of a professional to give me a call and I would connect them to who they needed. I ended up becoming a great connector. Within six months, I was getting as many calls from people who had other needs as I was from people who needed limousine service.

Are you thinking that sounds like a lot of work? Are you thinking, "Why would I do that?" Simple, as the great Zig Ziglar is known for saying, "You can have everything in life you want; if you just help other people get what they want." Mary, a limousine client, bought a new house. As I was driving her home from the airport, she asked me if I knew a good painter for her foyer. I told Mary I would have the painter give her a call. She told me that would be great, and she walked into her house.

I called a painter I knew named John. I explained the need my client had and asked him to call my client and let me know once the job was completed. Three days later, John called and told me he just finished the job and that Mary seemed really happy.

I then called Mary and asked her how the job went. She was very happy and couldn't believe how I called her back so swiftly. I told

Mary that she means a lot to me and I am never too busy for her. A week later, Mary had a housewarming party. Four of her friends asked where she found the painter. She told them about what I had done. Her friends were so amazed, I picked up four corporate accounts from them.

Building a successful business doesn't happen overnight, nor is it difficult. Over the years, I have continued to study many successful entrepreneurs who built both traditional and non-traditional businesses. I have noticed the secret to their success really came down to a few key points.

The six lessons every small business owner should follow:

Lesson 1:
Identify your target market – Who is your ideal customer?

Lesson 2:
Identify your Competitive Edge – What are your core strengths which sets you apart from your competition?

Lessons 3:
Identify your Value Proposition - Why should someone do business with you instead of someone else?

Lesson 4:
When building a business, build a financial asset not just a job – What is the true value of your business after five years?

Lesson 5:
Focus on your *Why*, while being a resource for your clients – What is your mission or purpose behind what you do?

Lesson 6:
Find a more non-traditional approach for how you build your business – Be careful your business doesn't just blend in with all the other businesses similar to yours.

I was talking with Claire O'Malley, an aspiring entrepreneur in her own right. When asked what she believes is an important quality a small business owner should possess, this is what she shared, "To prosper, a business doesn't only survive on the latest technology, a monopoly on low prices, or even the most avant-garde idea; it needs a brilliant mind who can ensure that none of its peers will think smarter, into the fine-print ways to succeed" (Claire O'Malley, personal communications, June 20, 2018).

Businesses come and go. The great ones grow into amazing companies and many disappear into the passages of time. In the end, it's often the non-traditional businesses which leave their mark and blaze a path for others to follow. It's great to be in business for yourself; however, you should never feel like you're by yourself.

Learn to champion your unique differences. And, as referenced by James O'Malley, founder of Brazilianaire.net, "Don't just give your business undivided attention, rather give your business the undivided intention it deserves" (personal communications, June 25, 2018). And in time, you will see your business soar to great heights – ultimately empowering you to discover your own true north and live the life you deserve.

Discovering Your Business's True North
Glossary:

Aspirations: The hopes of achieving something.

Avant-garde: New and unusual or experimental ideas.

CEO: Chief executive officer, the highest-ranking person in a company or other institution, ultimately responsible for making managerial decisions.

CFO: Chief financial officer, a senior executive with responsibility for the financial affairs of a corporation or other institution.

Competitive edge: Your core strengths which set you apart from your competition.

Dilemma: When a situation requires a difficult choice between two or more alternatives.

Entrepreneurs: A person who organizes and operates a business or businesses, taking on greater than normal financial risks in order to do so.

Financial asset: A non-physical asset whose value is derived from a contractual claim, such as bank deposits, bonds, and stocks. Financial assets are usually more liquid than other tangible assets and may be traded on financial markets.

Fundraiser: Fundraising or fund raising is the process of gathering voluntary contributions of money or other resources.

Monopoly: In economics, a monopoly is a single seller. In law, a monopoly is a business entity that has significant market power, that is, the power to charge overly high prices.

Networking: An effective low-cost marketing method for

developing sales opportunities and contacts, based on referrals and introductions.

Non-traditional: People or things that don't follow accepted beliefs and behavior. Inventing new ways of doing things is being non-traditional.

Organization: An organized body of people with a particular purpose, especially a business, society, association, etc.

Outside of the box: A metaphor that means to think differently, unconventionally, or from a new perspective.

Point of valuation: The determination of the true value of a business. The point at which the business would sell for in the open market.

Professional chauffeurs: In general, most chauffeurs either own their own vehicle or drive as an employee for a private company.

Prototype: A first or preliminary model of something.

Recognition: The action or process of being acknowledged.

Re-examined: To rethink a topic.

Referrals: An introduction of one person or business to another person or business.

Saturated market: When a product has become diffused (distributed) within a market.

Target market: A particular group of consumers at which a product or service is aimed.

Technology: The application of scientific knowledge for practical purposes, especially in industry. Commonly referred to via the computer industry.

True north: Following one's heart or staying true to your purpose.

Undivided intention: Ultimate focus. Focusing on what's most important and not getting side-tracked.

Value proposition: (In marketing) an innovation, service, or feature intended to make a company or product attractive to customers.

Meet Brilliant Practicing Expert™ Mike Raber:

#1 Bestselling Author | Business Mentor | Financial Coach

Mike Raber is a #1 Amazon Bestselling Author, Speaker, and Coach. Mike's skills and capabilities of leadership, financial planning, real estate, building relationships, growing different businesses, and writing a book with his daughter on the secret to raising financial savvy kids has helped make him the father and business coach that he is today. "Mike knows people, especially the concerns of our youth." Some have said he's the *Millennial Mentor*. You'll be glad you took time to meet Mike.

MIKE'S SPECIAL INVITATION FOR YOU:

Free access to a variety of business development resources: Go to **www.MicroBizCorp.com/**

Micro Business Corporation

Business: Micro Business Corp.

In business and in life, we are rewarded for what do; yet, are often paid for what we know. In business, income will only rise to the level of one's knowledge or self-esteem.

Welcome to Micro Biz Corp's Centsible Solutions. Where you can experience a three-tiered platform to support your business's growth. The three tiers are: Mindset, Business Development, and Financial. We support business owners in designing their solid business foundation, which creates flexibility and freedom. Additionally, we've created a community to support and sustain success.

Website: http://www.MicroBizCorp.com/

Connect with Mike on this social account:
LinkedIn: https://www.linkedin.com/in/mikeraber
Author Profile: **amazon.com/author/mikeraber**

Download Mobile App: BrilliantBizBook from your App Store. It contains everything related to this Book Series and its Authors.

Brilliant Breakthroughs for the Small Business Owner

Allow Me to Introduce Brilliant Practicing Expert™
Susan White, by Maggie Mongan

Susan is an exceptional therapist, who has a Small Business background. I appreciate her very practical approach. We've known each other for 7 or 8 years and every conversation we have is phenomenal. Allow me to explain.

Susan impresses me with her gift to deeply listen to what people are really saying. She doesn't respond with preconceived cookie-cutter Q&A. She keeps her conversations real and focused.

Susan has another gift – she is a master of *Shadow Work*. Directly trained by the late Debbie Ford, Susan continues to deliver breakthroughs to her clients in unexpected fashion. Her understanding of how our Shadow can work for or against us is expansive.

Susan's chapter will take you on a journey of the actual willingness, success perceptions, and realities of several Small Business Owners, who openly share their truths and realities.

As you journey with your colleagues, this chapter will have you contemplating your own willingness and perceptions of success. This self-awareness will support your success.

Are You Willing to be Successful?
by Susan White

A former boss of mine had a tin can sitting on his desk. It was fully-sealed and had a label in bold black letters that read, "Success Comes in Cans!" He informed me it was a gift from a colleague. It impacted me immediately the first time I saw it, and I've never forgotten it. It was symbolic of having a "can-do" (pun-intended) attitude, as well as having a positive view point.

Whether you are positive or negative will certainly influence success, but the real question is: Are you willing to be successful? Before we explore your resounding "yes" answer, let's look at the concept of success, as well as willingness, to see what they both mean.

Define Success

As a business owner, have you ever thought, "I need an extra day to myself between Saturday and Sunday?" What about those times when our bills exceed our bank account? Don't we all wish we had extra cash on hand? Some of us crave recognition for a job well done, or a simple acknowledgement for the passion we pour into our craft. How do you want to fill your days and evenings? Is it with more interaction or in solitude?

Do you willingly rise to a challenge or do you prefer to play it safe? These questions are posed in a quest to get a handle on what "success" means. Is it some kind of *happily ever after* cliché, or is it something else to you? Don't most people have a pretty clear idea of what success is? I'm going to suggest the answer lies in murky waters of illusion and others' definitions of the concept. I urge you to develop your own concept of success as you continue reading.

Success Variations

In my research regarding success, I have uncovered a variety of themes, definitions, and measurements. Some of these are my own, but I have also been pleasantly surprised by how others perceive and define success. What has surprised me most about success is that I can easily relate to a piece of each premise I've uncovered. One thing is for sure, anyone who embarks on beginning a business, or already has a business, hopes for success!

Kimberly Allain, High Performance Coach, states, "Success is the fruit of hope in action." She expounds on that brief definition by stating, "It [success] is defined by my conscious choice of showing up as my highest and best self and interacting with everyone around me in that space so that I am a positive contagion in the world. If I can do that, then that's success. Everything else is the fruit of those relationships" (personal communications, August 26, 2018). What a powerful definition. I've never heard the word *contagion* used in such a positive light!

When I hear Kimberly's definition of success, I automatically reflect upon self-satisfaction as a measurement. I am not referring to self-serving satisfaction, but rather that *sitting on top of a rainbow feeling* we have when we are true to ourselves and acting in integrity. What a powerful place to be!

Debbie Leoni, Fearless Life Coach and author of "I am Fearless: 12 Elements of Fearless Living," defines success as "living a fulfilled life and living on purpose." She goes on to add, "Ultimately, it comes down to really living your passion based on your God-given talents, dreams, and desires." She continued with, "Success is right here in this moment and it's possible for anyone." Finally, Debbie was clear that a definition for success is not one-size-fits-all, but each person needs to define it for him or herself.

She acknowledged how important it is to "love yourself fully, which in turn allows you to love others fully" (personal communications, August 27, 2018). Pouring love into my own business is part of my recipe for success. This makes sense to me.

Stacy Kaat, Owner of Stacy Kaat Photography, relishes the small successes like checking tasks off her to-do list. This helps her give her an ability to plan and a sense of control over her life, as well as her business. It also eliminates worry. Stacy has not always defined success as completion of the little things. Five years ago, she defined success as monetary until she was able to pay herself. Now she realizes, "people weave in and out of success mode." She says "I used to think once I was successful, that would be it... Like, I arrived!"

She further revealed, "Success ebbs and flows, consistently evolving, as well as redefining itself as we change our minds about what success means." In short, without expansion and contraction, we won't individually develop and neither will our businesses.

Stacy also defines success as doing one thing well and not focusing on too many other things at once. At times, when she's gotten caught up in too many directions, she found she didn't perform well in any one area. In addition to spinning her wheels, she ended up frustrated.

Stacy shared, "New business owners often try to be everything to everybody with the intention that filling everybody's needs will bring them success. That doesn't work. That's the power in branding and knowing what you do well. Specializing in something very specific is powerful" (personal communications, August 26, 2018).

Wealth

Acquiring wealth has long been a primary benchmark for measuring success. Of course, there are a proliferation of clichés framing money in a negative light, as well as positive. It's not my intention to exploit or explore the obvious. We need money to live in society, and any successful business needs to have a positive cash flow.

My own formula for financial success is quite simple. First, I keep my overhead low so I can retain more of my earnings. Secondly, I surround myself with good people and allow them to do their jobs. Lastly, and probably most significant, I love what I do for a living and get a great deal of self-satisfaction from my work.

Kimberly Allain and I discussed money during an interview. "It [money] is an interesting thing. Money is a wonderful thing. Having financial freedom is a wonderful thing, but it's the fruit of something, it's not the thing. If the focus is on money, then truly... how do we go about getting it?"

Further, she referenced money as an "external validation," as well as sharing another perspective of money as a tool – which mirrors my own viewpoint on money. Most significant about our conversation was the clarity with which Kimberly reverted right back to her core values as a means of gaining wealth.

Notwithstanding, I believe successful people make money NOT because that is their primary focus, but rather they attract money to themselves because of other attributes or values.

Luck

How much does luck influence success? According to the Roman Philosopher, Seneca, "Luck Is What Happens When Preparation Meets Opportunity." This is one of my favorite quotes and reminds me how what we say, and do, has a significant impact on outcome in our lives long before we become successful.

I use my own life as an example. Prior to my calling as a clinical social worker, I was a Mortgage Loan Originator. I spent years reviewing tax returns and balance sheets, as well as profit and loss statements. I developed an understanding of self-employment and what it entailed in terms of qualifying for a mortgage.

When it came time to hang my own shingle, it was less intimidating due to the knowledge I had acquired, and I had a pretty clear understanding of what I was getting into. After the first three months or so, it was an easy transition for me. I attribute that easy transition to self-employment to my Mortgage Banking years.

Whenever anyone says, "You are so lucky..." I just smile. How are you lucky? What experiences or skills do you have which contribute to your current success?

Self-Satisfaction

Most of us say we want success, but are we willing to go to any lengths to be successful? Stacy Kaat has come to some newfound notions about her own achievement. When her photography business became successful and she was acquiring clients through word of mouth referrals and exposure of her work, she found herself mourning the loss of her free time. She was thrilled her investment in marketing had paid off both in terms of income and exposure. However, her former life had given her opportunities to engage in personal hobbies that "nourished her soul." Grateful for increased revenue, she longed for the days of working in her garden to produce vegetables for canning.

While Stacy is clear about the self-satisfaction her craft provides, she reframed success and now buys vegetables at the local farmer's market. She has traded one value for another and now helps support local farmers and enjoys meandering among the vendors – ultimately finding it relaxing.

She also carves out personal time in her schedule and sets time aside in her calendar, so she doesn't become overwhelmed or burned-out. It's quite simple, you can't recharge a non-rechargeable battery and it's important to schedule "me time" for us all.

Constant Growth

Constant growth is a standard of success. In my mind, constant growth means changing the way we may go about doing things, but not the values or intention with which we do them. I am

139

reminded of a millennial client I worked with who had a difficult time holding a conversation. Can you imagine how painful a traditional talk therapy session would be for such a client?

After spending two very challenging sessions for both of us and exchanging several texts, it occurred to me perhaps texting might be more effective than traditional talk therapy. Not commonly endorsed, this method of initially conducting therapy got us to a place where we became familiar with one another and could eventually have a conversation easily.

If I had not been willing to change how I went about conducting myself, this client may never have gotten the attention he needed. In business, we always need to be thinking along the lines of *how to* accomplish an objective, rather than limiting ourselves or doing things the way they have always been done.

Failure

I would be remiss not to address failure, since it is extremely valuable to success. Who would knowingly undertake a new endeavor intending to fail? No one I know! Fear of failure will shut down any hope of success faster than anything else I can think of. How many people have dreams, which lay dormant due to fear of failure?

At times, failure can be a positive thing – depending on what you do with it. Isn't failure one of life's greatest teachers? It teaches us what behaviors and actions not to take in the future. It teaches resiliency and it can also stretch us into meeting our highest potential. If you doubt how powerful failure can be, do an internet search to see how many wildly successful people were once failures!

Debbie Leoni does not buy into the concept of failure and states, "It's only failure if there's no learning and there's a pattern that results in people not getting what they want most. The value in failure is the opportunity to learn and grow." Whatever you do, don't ever allow either failure, or fear of failure, to stop you from pursuing your dreams. After all, isn't reality built on dreams?

Investing in Success

Progressive small business owners invest in themselves, as well as their businesses. Stacy Kaat referred at length to how valuable professional organizations are to both personal growth, as well as her business's success. As a result of networking and professional affiliations, she has "stretched and grown in thousands of ways that she can't even describe." Not to mention, Stacy credits the photographer who did her own head shot as a valuable learning experience and resource.

First hand, she saw how someone else did what she does and gained valuable insight into being a consumer of professional headshot services. That specific experience helped her realize competencies she never would have acknowledged otherwise. She also recognized how networking helps to differentiate uniqueness in any given profession. Finally, Stacy credits hiring and working with a business coach as being invaluable. She described herself as being wholehearted – a direct result of all the work she has invested into her own success.

Working Success

It's unrealistic to believe that you will be an overnight success in business. Is it possible? Yes. Is it probable? No.

While being an overnight success may sound appealing, there's immense value to be gained in taking time to grow and evolve with your small business. When we learn something new, we need to contemplate how it may or may not benefit us. Additionally, once we engage in a new way of doing things, it takes us some time to be in relationship with the new behavior to create a sense of comfort and trust.

Business development is as important as hiring the right people to do the right job and having a dream. Debbie Leoni discussed how she "added patience and trust" to her business plan. She concluded, "I wanted things to happen faster than they did. I put a lot of pressure on myself." Use your time wisely while your business grows and evolves through stages of change. It will benefit both you and your business.

Is success synonymous with hard work? You bet it is! However, that doesn't mean it's hard to be successful. On the contrary, it can be quite simple. Most small business owners are hard workers and all three people I interviewed agree that if you aren't willing to invest the time in yourself, you are spinning your wheels.

Debbie Leoni shared, "Willingness and commitment are similar. In order to be willing to be a success, you've got to be committed." In short, commitment and willingness go hand in hand. Debbie continues, "Willingness is not always about passion. It's doing something even when you don't feel like doing it. Willingness requires that you're in the reality of your situation."

When it comes to success, a resounding theme is those who are successful are led by their core values, or rather their core values are foundational in all that they say and do. There needs to be some delegation of duties so we are not overwhelmed and frustrated. We need to be interdependent with others. We need to be patient and set realistic goals. Above all, we need to honor our core values and have the self-awareness to shift gears when you go into fear mode. We need to have hope and take action. Doing all that will assure likelihood of success.

As we become clear about what it means to be successful and can give it meaning with our hearts, as well as our minds, that wisdom will lead and guide us every step of the way. Individual heartfelt meaning eliminates the need to embrace some random, subjective notion of success, and we can revel in knowing that we just may have been successful all along.

Are You Willing to be Successful?
Glossary:

Commitment: To pledge or obligate oneself; to be responsible or to entrust.

Concept: Something conceived in the mind; in the abstract or generic idea constructed from individual thought, perception, or experience.

Core values: The innermost qualities of a person regarded as desirable or worthwhile; qualities of value.

External validation: To receive a sense of important value outside of oneself.

Hope: A feeling of expectation and desire for a certain thing to happen; grounds for believing something may happen to help or save someone or something.

Integrity: The quality of being honest with oneself, as well as others, and having strong moral and ethical principles; sincerity, truthfulness, and trustworthiness.

Investment: A quality of value placed in a person, place or thing with the expectation of future benefit.

Passion: A powerful feeling of great enthusiasm.

Progressive: Moving forward; advancing in taking continuous steps by stages or degrees.

Quality: Essential character trait or nature of a person.

Success: The achievement of something desired, intended, or attempted; the gaining of fame or prosperity.

Willingness: The quality of acting or responding promptly; readiness to act or giving voluntarily.

Meet Brilliant Practicing Expert™ Susan White:

Licensed Clinical Social Worker | Integrative Life Coach

Susan White, MSW, LCSW and Integrative Life Coach, has worked in the Corporate World, Retail Management and Human Services. She's long been fascinated by personal transformation and human resilience – especially in the face of adversity. In 1993, she was told, "You've done well for someone with a substandard education." That back-handed compliment inspired her to pursue a BA from Judson College (1996) and MSW from Aurora University, George Williams School of Social Work (2001). Susan lives in her hometown of Antioch, IL with her husband and black lab, although she's lived in various locations throughout the Chicagoland area as well.

SUSAN'S SPECIAL INVITATION FOR YOU:

Explore what success means to your small business and reap the rewards. Receive clarity today: **http://www.lifeskillsctr.com/**

Lifeskills Center, Ltd.

Business: Lifeskills Center, Ltd.

After working at several non-profit agencies reliant on government funding, Susan White, MSW, LCSW, decided to create her own small business dedicated to helping people transform their lives. In January 2007, Susan founded, Lifeskills Center, Ltd. in Antioch, IL. There, she helps adults face financial, relational or career concerns, mental health issues, divorce, death or any personal difficulties. Susan says, "We all face challenges we don't want to encounter, although viewing them as 'life experiences' often provides hidden opportunities to learn, grow and develop. That is the core of what Lifeskills Center and my work is all about."

Website: http://www.lifeskillsctr.com/

Connect with Susan on these social accounts:
Facebook: https://www.facebook.com/Lifeskills-Center-Ltd-331914257290/
Psychology Today: https://therapists.psychologytoday.com/rms/prof_detail.php?profid=72780&p=1
Author Profile: **https://amazon.com/author/white_s**

Download Mobile App: BrilliantBizBook from your App Store. It contains everything related to this Book Series and its Authors.

Brilliant Breakthroughs for the Small Business Owner

CONCLUSION

By now, I'm sure you noticed our team of Brilliant Practicing Experts™ is overflowing with best practices and unconventional approaches to help you succeed in 21st century small business success.

We hope you have built a plan (strategy) to take actions from whichever chapters will best serve you now. Each quarter, come back and find some more techniques to improve your business's performance.

REMEMBER: This book is dedicated to you. It is designed to make your job easier. The only thing I'd like to add is how to make this book work for you:

- Apply the strategies and techniques discussed here.
- Accept each author's invitations on their Author Page.
- Engage with the authors via their social media accounts.
- Download our Free Mobile App: **BrilliantBizBook** Why? Each author will have extra and ongoing support there for you through weekly podcasts, blogs, videos, and events.
- Go to amazon.com and let us know what you found useful and then let us know what you'd like to learn in our 2019 book.

START HERE: Get your ROI out of the book by following the above checklist and begin shining brightly! Then, go back to 2017's #1 Bestselling book (Volume 1 in this series) and begin applying its different and fresh perspectives. If you do this, you'll be ready for when we roll out Volume 3 (November 2019).

Brilliant Breakthroughs for the Small Business Owner

AUTHORS' COLLECTIVE BIBLIOGRAPHY:

Accelity Marketing, Steinmetz, Jackie (2018, June 12). Personal Communication [Telephone interview].

ActionCOACH Business Coaching (Southeast Wisconsin), Palzewicz, Max (2018, June 27). Personal Communication [Telephone interview].

Allain Solutions.us, Allain, Kimberly (2018, August 26). Personal Communication [Telephone Interview].

An, M. (2017). *State of Inbound 2017* [PDF]. Boston: Hubspot.

Arianna Huffington. *Why a Nap Room is So Important at Work.* Retrieved July 5, 2018, from https://www.architecturaldigest.com/story/thrive-nap-room-cocomat-arianna-huffington

Behind Your Curtain, LLC, Albert, Karen (2018, September 4). Personal Communication [Email Interview].

Bennett, Milton, 2013, Overcoming the Golden Rule: *Sympathy and empathy*, (2nd. Ed.). Boston, MA: Intercultural Press.

Brazilianaire.net, O'Malley, James (2018, June 25). Personal Communication [Interview].

Burchard, B. (2017). *High Performance Habits: How Extraordinary People Become That Way.* California: Hay House Inc.

Chopra, D. (2018). *The Healing Self.* New York: Harmony Books.
Covey, Steven, (2008). *The SPEED of Trust: The One Thing that Changes Everything*, Free Press, Simon & Schuster, New York.

Debbie Leoni, (2018, August 27). Personal Communication [Telephone Interview].

Deepak Chopra. Retrieved July 5, 2018, from https://en.wikipedia.org/wiki/Deepak_Chopra

Deming, Edward, (1982). *Out of the Crisis,* MIT Press, Cambridge, MA.

DRCS Solutions, Rebro, Dave (2018, July 27). Personal Communication [Telephone Interview].

Dubetz, Meina (2018, August 28). Personal Communication [Telephone Interview].

Dwyer, Charles, (1991). *The shifting sources of power and influence*, Wharton School of Business, American College of Physician Executives.

Elite Online Publishing, Foster, Jenn (2018, September 3). Personal Communication [Interview].

Everything is Energy and That's All There Is to It. Match the Frequency of The Reality You Want. Retrieved July 5, 2018, from https://quoteinvestigator.com/2012/05/16/everything-energy/

FocalPoint Business Coaching, A Hoffman Advantage LLC, Hoffman, Kerrie (2018, September 4). Personal Communication [Telephone Interview].

Global View Capital Advisors, Fliss, Dean (2018, July 11). Personal Communication [Interview].

Hammond, Charmaine (2018, August 30). Personal Communication [Interview].

Herbworks, Drummer, Roger (2018, June 6). Personal Communication [Video Interview].

Ignite Press, O'Keefe, Everett (2018 August 31). Personal Communication [Interview].

James, Henry,(n.d.). BrainyQuote.com. Retrieved August 19, 2018, from BrainyQuote.com Web site: https://www.brainyquote.com/quotes/henry_james_157155

Join the Self-Care Revolution. Module 1: Thoughts and Food as Medicine. Retrieved July 5, 2018 from http://robynbenson.com/wp-content/uploads/2017/08/Module01_02_Body_Text.pdf

Kerpen, D. (2017). *The art of people: 11 simple people skills that will get you everything you want*. London: Portfolio Penguin.

Lipton, B. (2005). *The Biology of Belief. Unleashing the Power of Consciousness, Matter and Miracles*. California: Hay House Inc.

Marr, B. (2018, May 21). How Much Data Do We Create Every Day? The Mind-Blowing Stats Everyone Should Read [Editorial]. *Forbes.com*. Retrieved from https://www.forbes.com/sites/bernardmarr/2018/05/21/how-much-data-do-we-create-every-day-the-mind-blowing-stats-everyone-should-read/#3e65a25a60ba

Nightingale, Earl. (1950). The Strangest Secret. [Audio].

O'Malley, Claire (2018, June 20). Personal Communication [Interview].

O'Malley, James (2018, June 25). Personal Communication [Interview].

PhysicsForums.com, Bernhardt, Greg (2018, June 7). Personal Communication [Telephone interview].

Priority Retreats, Polowczuk, Lora (2018, July 27). Personal Communication [Telephone Interview].

Quantum Leap Coaching, Alvarez, Amira (2018, June 11). Personal Communication [Telephone interview].

Raveworthy, Mulrennan, Mia (2018, June 14). Personal Communication [Video Interview].

Salveo Partners, Ward, Rosie (June 12, 2018). Personal Communication [Video Interview].

Shealy, N. (2010). *Energy Medicine: Practical Applications and Scientific Proof.* Virginia: 4th Dimension Press.

Sinek, S. (2009). *Start with why: how great leaders inspire everyone to take action.* London: Portfolio/Penguin.

Sonia Choquette. Youtube videos. (2018, March1). Retrieved July 5, 2018, from https://www.youtube.com/watch?v=jiB8WtnA4Ic

Stacy Kaat Photography, Kaat, Stacy (2018, August 26). Personal Communication [Telephone Interview].

The Third Metric - The two Steps to Solving our Real Energy Crisis. Retrieved July 5, 2018, from https://drhyman.com/blog/2013/06/03

Vichen Lakhaini. Youtube video. (Nov. 3, 2106). Retrieved July 5, 2018, from https://www.youtube.com/watch?v=tddzKkTzFUA&feature=youtu.beSelfTranscendence

Wings of Freedom, Higgins, Maureen (2018, June 20). Personal Communication [Video Interview].

Wisdom to Wealth Mastery, Ferreira, Sue (2018, September 7). Personal Communication [Interview].

Made in the USA
Middletown, DE
04 July 2019